ENGLAND
MY LOVE

14th June, 2014

HER MAJESTY THE QUEEN

has been pleased to confer

The British Empire Medal (Civil Division)

upon

Mr. Dharam Bir Lall

Registrar,
The Order of the British Empire

ENGLAND MY LOVE

Bill Lall

STERLING

STERLING PAPERBACKS
An imprint of
Sterling Publishers (P) Ltd.
Regd. Office: A1/256 Safdarjung Enclave,
New Delhi-110029. CIN: U22110DL1964PTC211907
Tel: 26387070, 26386209
E-mail: mail@sterlingpublishers.in
www.sterlingpublishers.in

England My Love
© 2018, Bill Lall
ISBN 978 93 86245 10 6

All rights are reserved.
No part of this publication may be reproduced, stored in a retrieval system or transmitted, in any form or by any means, mechanical, photocopying, recording or otherwise, without prior written permission of the publisher.

Printed and Published in India by

Sterling Publishers Pvt. Ltd.,
Plot No. 13, Ecotech-III, Greater Noida - 201306, U. P. India

Acknowledgements

To my dear wife Shashi, darling daughter Deesha and my sweet granddaughter Lusha, who have given me strength and support all the way.

To my brother Baldev and his wife Sheila, who supported me financially in the early stages of life; but for them I would not be where I am today.

To Paul Diner, a perfect English gentleman, who has provided help and guidance in preparing this book.

To Achal Paul for his excellent work on the design and layout of the book.

To Jaya Lall and Simran Kaur, for their secretarial and general assistance.

Finally, I am most grateful to Mr. S.K. Ghai, Managing Director Sterling Publishers Pvt. Ltd., for taking personal interest in publishing the book.

1

Falling in Love with England: Who Am I?

> I travelled among unknown men,
> In lands beyond the sea:
> Nor England! Did I know till then
> What love I bore to thee.
>
> William Wordsworth

I am an Indian immigrant and came to England in 1959 during the 'high-wave era' of immigration. I only had a few pounds in my pocket when I arrived.

I have been in England now for more than half a century—longer than I lived in my mother country. So, in every sense, England has now become my home and I love it more than any other country in the world.

During this time, my life and character have changed dramatically, both materially and mentally. I feel proud of what I have achieved during these years. All my successes have been achieved by following the principles described in my previous two books. I do not wish to blow my own trumpet, but I think it is essential for you to know that, having arrived with only a few pounds in my pocket, I now live today in a large detached house in one of the most exclusive suburbs of London. I drive a Jaguar, which bears my personalised number plate. I built and ran my business, employing 14 staff and I also own properties that bring me additional income.

I was the first person from an ethnic business community to get elected as the Chair of Newham Chamber of Commerce (in East London) in its 100 years of existence and was awarded an Honorary Doctorate of Business Administration by the University of East London in 2003. I was also awarded the British Empire Medal in the Queen's Birthday Honours List of 2014.

Well, things were not all that rosy when I arrived in England. I came to London on May 1st, 1959. In fact, at that time, it was practically impossible to find a room in a respectable English family home. Notices in shop windows read, 'Room available, sorry no coloured, no Irish, no dogs'. All sorts of prejudices were rife. To some extent they are still there and I have described them in detail in one of the chapters in this book.

One evening, a few days after arrival, I was walking through Hyde Park in complete desperation. My pockets were empty, except for one shilling. I was lonely. I saw courting couples around me enjoying themselves on that beautiful, sunny, May evening, while I had nothing to live on. Tears started streaming from my eyes. I cried for hours and hours. I longed for my homeland.

Eventually, a Jewish accountancy firm in Manchester accepted me as an articled clerk. I worked hard for a period of five years and qualified as a chartered accountant in 1964. This was an achievement. I felt as if I had reached the pinnacle of my life. During those years of study, I had lived in small, seedy digs, mostly run by Irish, Polish or Jewish immigrants.

After qualifying, I moved to Birmingham, where I worked for a year for a large firm of chartered accountants, Peat, Marwick, Mitchell & Co. (now KPMG). I then left to join Dunlop, the tyre manufacturers, where I stayed for four years. I was still not happy.

Soon, I realised that becoming a chartered accountant did not fulfil my ambitions. I felt frustrated, so I decided to leave England, altogether, and look for a brighter future on fresh soil.

I packed my belongings, left for Milan in Italy and worked there for a year with Price Waterhouse (now PWC), an international firm of chartered accountants. However, the change of country and employer did not bring any new happiness or the wealth that I had been seeking since I was a child. That great life about which I had been dreaming had not yet come to me, although I had worked hard so far and had moved from one country to another in search of that all-embracing happiness.

This is the particular point that I emphasised in my previous two books—*Rich Man Happy Man* and *How to Grow Rich and Enjoy Life*—that happiness and wealth are within you. You might move from one place to another, or from one country to another, but until and unless you realise the real truth behind wealth and happiness, you will not achieve them. You can achieve whatever you want, irrespective of who you are or where you were born. It was not just leaving my land of birth that secured my future—it was the principles I followed, most of which I learnt in England, that made me rich and happy.

I packed my bags again and returned to good old England.

I was now married, and started looking for a secure job. I secured a position as a senior accountant with the Ministry of Defence and I became a civil servant. It was 1970, and my wife was expecting a baby. I had bought a small town house just outside London. I felt I was now settled in England, like a middle-class English person—a secure job, my own house on a mortgage, a wonderful wife and a little baby. I would travel to the city in the morning, start work at 9, finish at 5, have a drink on the way back home in a pub, read an evening paper while having my drink, come home, eat, play with the baby, and then slump into an easy chair before the television and start dozing off. A typical English Babu's life!

I hoped to rise to a high position in the Civil Service, but soon realised that my ambitions were to be thwarted. I was called to a few promotion interviews, but had no success.

In February 1974, I was called to another interview for promotion to a chief accountant's post. I was confident that I would be selected this time. On 28th February 1974, Edward Heath lost the general election on the issue of the miners' strike and Harold Wilson was returned as the Prime Minister. That very day, I learned the result of my interview, that I had lost my chance of the promotion of which I had been so confident. So had Heath, I suppose.

I left the office early and wandered through Hyde Park and then to the streets of Soho. It was exactly as I had done 15 years before, when I had first arrived in this country, looking for articles and no one in London would take me on. Rejected, dejected, tears streaming from my eyes, I bought a ticket to a seedy Soho cinema club. I sat, slept and cried in that cinema until closing time.

I was on the horns of a dilemma. Should I carry on with my Civil Service career and continue fighting for promotion, or just quit, once and for all, and start something afresh? I had to decide what I really wanted out of life. I could carry on working as a civil servant with a secure job, home and family, or did I want something much more than that?

No. I wanted something more in life. I reflected deeply that day. If I stayed as a civil servant, I would have remained a civil servant for the rest of my life. If I kept trying for a promotion, I might become a principal one day.

But after getting one promotion, I would soon be back in the same situation, that is, fighting for another promotion to senior principal, and so on. This vicious circle would continue churning my dreams of prosperity into paste. Whatever happened, I would still be a civil servant. Then I compared myself with many other Asians, who were immigrants as I was, who were doing better than me. They were driving expensive cars and living better lives than I did.

That was it. My desire from childhood had been to become rich, make money and enjoy life, live like my rich uncles lived, live like my rich brother lived in India. So I said to myself, 'I am not going to live a middle-class family life for the rest of my days. I want to be something. *I want to be a millionaire!*'

As a civil servant, I thought to myself, I could never become a millionaire. At that very moment, I decided that I was going to be an independent, rich person, and avail myself of all the enjoyments of life that money brings with it. With these thoughts simmering inside me, I returned home a different person. My mind was full of new desires, ambitions and aspirations. All these principles are described in my other two books.

Apart from achieving wealth and a comfortable life over the years, apart from the struggles and prejudices that I came across, and apart from the fact that in the early years I longed to go back to the land of my birth, over the years England started growing in me so much so that if somebody now asked me to go back to India, my answer would be emphatically, 'No!' As much as I love India, England is now my home.

Over the period of 60 years so many changes have taken place in England, indeed in the world all over, and so have I changed with my England. As the days and years have gone by, a sort of spiritual love has developed within me for my England. Exactly as when you fall in love with someone, you find a source of love in every aspect of that person, so my love for England grew. No, I will not and will not want to leave this great country, great people, great weather, great facilities, great respect for human lives. I just love England madly.

My love for England grew and deepened over the years. I once met an Australian who told me then when he first landed in Calcutta, India, he just fell in love with India. He adopted Indian clothes, Indian habits and Indian religion and he became a follower of the Hare Rama Hare Krishna movement. Later, he was sent by his guru in Calcutta to England to spread the message of the movement abroad. He devoted himself fully to that mission, he even wrote books in Bengali. He was completely in love with India and his love was at first sight.

My love for England, on the other hand, grew as time passed. I just started loving the English manner, English culture, English politics, and English etiquette—all of which I enjoy very much, having become a part of it all. And I describe all this in this book.

As the time passed, I analysed in my mind English habits, culture, traditions, and from all aspects, including the overall beauty of this island. On the top of it all, I read a lot of books on different subjects relating to England and the English way life. I ultimately crystallised all my thoughts and observations in this book.

Once again, I emphasise that everything I say or feel in this book relates to my lovable England. It is England where I have lived all these 60 years. I know that in this country as well as in India, there are people who deprecate England for carrying out cruelties in India. To those people I would say that firstly these cruelties were nowhere near the inhuman cruelties that were carried out by other rulers. I tell my friends in India that roads having English names should not be changed. The English did a lot for India. They modernised our country and had they ruled another 60 years, India today would have been a different country altogether.

Any cruelty and misbehaviour that was carried out appears to have been by the British and not the English. There seems to be some sort of evidence that it was the Irish, Scottish and Welsh who carried out most of these atrocities. They probably suffered an inferiority complex compared to the English and when they got to India they amassed unexpectedly great power and they enjoyed being cruel and nasty to the local people. On the other hand, true English people who came to India seemed to behave with dignity, respecting and admiring the beauty of that country and did so much good to that country.

The various chapters in this book represent my feelings and observations of the English people—to my mind, the greatest people on earth. I am sure you will enjoy reading them as much as I have enjoyed writing them.

2

The Legendary English Politeness

An Earl by right, by courtesy a man.

Alfred Austin

English Gentlemen and Ladies are unique human beings who, in my opinion, exist only in Good Old England. It took me a while to understand or recognise these types of human beings around me, but once I understood the deep meaning of this gentle behaviour, I took great pleasure in becoming a part of this tradition.

A perfect English Gentleman holds the door for you if you are behind him, unlike in India in my experience, during the course of my recent visits, where a person pushes past you. I did not go to India for nearly 45 years, but since retirement I have been going three to four times a year and staying at five-star hotels. The English gentleman lets you go first if he happens to be in front of you, irrespective of your age, sex, or colour; raises himself up if a lady enters the room; if walking with a lady on the street, he lets her stay on the curb side; talks softly; makes you feel comfortable if you are a stranger in the company; respects your culture, dress, manners, religion and so much more.

As a stranger, a somewhat shy and relatively boorish young man, completely new to the English ways of life, who first stepped on English soil at London's Victoria Station on 1st May 1959 (which was not a public holiday in those days), everything that I saw and experienced around me, at that moment, appeared as if coming straight from a fairy tale.

Compared to my country, everything looked different. Huge impressive buildings, an affluent life style, strange dresses were definitely expected, but beyond all, immaculate cleanliness and orderliness everywhere struck my mind instantly. Being a university graduate, I had surely expected this much difference between the living styles of well-developed and developing countries. What really surprised me was a striking contrast between the general mannerisms seen in England and those seen back home. Every person exuded an aura of a strange aloofness, maintaining a respectful distance from every other person. In addition to this, the instinctive politeness towards one and all surprised me beyond all expectations.

Having placed my few belongings in left luggage, I set about trying to find the only person I knew in the whole country—a very distant family connection, my brother's wife's cousin. I had his address, but where was it? With some trepidation I approached a policeman (we, in India, call them policemen but later on to my surprise I learnt that in this country, a policeman is addressed as a Police Officer) and asked for directions which he duly gave me, explaining precisely which bus I should catch and where to get off. I was astonished. He was so charming and polite and quite the opposite of what I had expected. Standing outside Victoria Station, at once I felt at ease.

Later on, after a few weeks, I arrived in Manchester, where I happened to get my first job. It was late evening when I got down at London Road station (the name of that station has now been changed to Piccadilly station). As I emerged from the station with my luggage, I was encountered by a tramp (those days, I did not know who and what tramp was) who asked me if I was looking for accommodation to which I replied, 'Yes.' He carried some of my luggage and took me to a nearby guest house, for which I suppose he got some money for introducing me to the place.

That place was run by a Polish lady. In those days, I had no idea of the distinction between Polish, Irish, Jews or other nationalities. I just felt or believed, in my naivety, that all white people were English. When I booked into this guest house, I notified the lady that the room was for 24 hours, as I would be looking for proper accommodation the following day. Whether or not she took any notice of what I said, she just booked me in and took my cash.

Next morning, I left the guest house, leaving my luggage behind, to look for the digs. Somebody told me that around the Victoria Park area there were large houses converted into digs, which were mainly lived in by students as the university was not far from there. I took a bus to Victoria Park, looked at notices in shop windows and jotted down a few addresses. I had learnt this technique of finding accommodation during the course of my four week stay in London. Then I knocked at various doors.

Ultimately, I managed to knock at the right door and got a room in a house owned by a Polish fellow. Those were the days of Rachman, when Polish people were getting involved in housing and were possibly exploiting the new wave of West Indian and Asian immigrants, who in later days got into this business themselves.

I paid my deposit and took the bus back to the guest house to collect my luggage. It was late that evening. The landlady would not let me have my luggage back unless I gave her one more day's rent as I had not booked out before 12 o'clock. I tried arguing with her that before booking in, I specifically mentioned that it would cover me for 24 hours. She just would not budge, so I went to the nearest Police Station. I explained my situation to a Police Officer, who listened to me very sympathetically and decided to come out with me to the guest house. He argued with the landlady on my behalf, but the lady would not budge from her position. I finally gave her the money and took my luggage. The Officer even helped me to carry it and on the way explained that if I wanted to pursue it further, I should go to court as it was a civil matter and that he was sorry that he was unable to help me in this case.

What struck me was the kindness, patience and politeness of these two Police Officers, in London and in Manchester, giving me directions and dealing with my problems with the landlady. As I was new to the country, these two Police Officers, who went out of their way to help me, left a lasting impression. Even though it is now so many years on, these two kindly faces stand out in my mind till this day.

At these moments it dawned on me that these English people considered every other human being as equal and treated them the way they would want to be treated themselves. Nobody jumped the queue and no one wanted to snatch another person's rights. Looking back, I now realise that I had also committed my first *faux pas*. I did not say 'thank you' to the Police Officers who were so kind and helpful to a stranger in their land.

Over the past nearly 60 years, I have come to realise that the English have turned politeness into an art form which serves a multitude of different purposes. As well as seeking to put their fellow citizens at their ease, it can also be a defence mechanism and a weapon. In conjunction with the infinite subtleties of the English language, it can be deployed to great effect in an infinite number of ways. But by and large, an English person is by inclination courteous. To paraphrase Cardinal John Newman, 'The definition of an English Gentleman is that he would never knowingly do harm to another.'

I should make it plain here that I am talking about the educated English people with whom mainly I had contact in my social and business life. I will touch on what has become the war-zone of what passes for everyday life among the less well-educated at the end. However, I have to be careful because I would not want to denigrate many of the much older generation who did not have the opportunity of a good education, but even without those benefits they had been taught by their parents what was right and to 'mind their manners'. A person well dressed, in sophisticated attire, may appear attractive to our eyes but it may not necessarily prove that he or she is a good person in terms of personal values. External trappings, in my opinion, are just like the clothes we wear and, at times, they can be an illusion. As much as a person cannot be judged on his or her inner qualities from the clothes they wear, a sweetly natured person cannot be judged as a good human being on the basis of external good manners. At the same time, the reverse is also true. A person devoid of articulated manners must not be construed as a bad person either.

While I do not attempt to present here a definitive guide to English good manners, sometimes it has to be said that what the English consider to be the done thing would strike many others as plain odd, to put it mildly.

The English, for example, are devoted to their animals, which often have free run of their house. Woe betide anyone who gets between an English person and their dog. Indeed, where else but in England would you get an expression like, 'Don't frighten the horses?' Roughly speaking, it means the English will forgive most bad behaviour, often specifically of a sexual nature, but quite literally you should not frighten the horses which they regard as second only to their dogs, probably followed in third place by their families. Of course, frightening horses can have catastrophic consequences, and can cause damage and danger to human life if they stampede, so there is a practicality behind this phrase.

Indians are generally polite in their own way and according to their own rules. There is of course a word for thank you but it is used sparingly. In restaurants it is not usual to thank waiters who bring you your food. Waiters are paid to serve the meal and it is not inherent in Indian culture to thank someone providing that sort of service. Again, I left India some 60 years ago, and did not return for nearly 45 years. During my recent visits, staying at 5-star hotels, I have noticed that people are using the words 'thank you' more often than in the days when I left India.

In England, when I started my first job in Manchester, I noticed that if I said 'thank you' for something, the other person also said 'thank you' back and that puzzled me for a while. Why are they saying 'thank you' to me? So, one day, I asked the secretary in the office where I was articled, why she had thanked me and she said because I had thanked her. That was something completely new to me. As a matter of fact, it is quite common for both parties to say thank you at the same time, although sometimes, you do hear the response 'you are welcome' or 'no problem' (although why it should be a problem is beyond me!). However, when I reflected philosophically on saying 'thank you' back, the logic of it dawned on me. I say it now all the time as a matter of habit.

Over the years I have realised that the politeness which exists in the English culture is exceptional. For anything that you say or do, they are always obliged to you and you receive back the phrase 'much obliged to you' and 'thank you very much indeed' and so on.

In the same way, in England everyone seems to apologise a lot, always saying 'sorry'. If I bump into someone in the street I always say 'sorry'. In India perhaps you would not but in England even the person you bump into will say sorry to you. I picked up this 'sorry' word very early on when I came to England and started using it myself. Next time you go into a shop in England just observe how many times you say 'sorry' and 'thank you' as you try and conduct a simple transaction; 'sorry' and 'thank you' as you move past people going into the store, 'thank you' as you get advice on finding something on the shelves and the repeated 'thank you' as you pay for your goods.

And that is a complete contrast to what you might come across in India in some shops or at stalls in a bazaar, where everyone seems to pass you by or push past you without saying 'sorry' or 'excuse me please'. Sales staff seldom say 'thank you' after they have taken your money. A few years ago, *Reader's Digest* carried out a survey on the culture of politeness and courtesy in all the major cities of the world. The researchers found that Delhi and Bombay were some of the lowest on the scale. An example quoted was: when one of the female researchers bought a pair of hair clips in a shop in Bombay, the male sales assistant turned his back on her as soon as she paid. When asked why he had not thanked her, the 31-year old was unapologetic, 'Madam, I am not an educated man. I hand goods over to the customers and that's it.'

I have also noticed that even in England, the second generation of young Indians is not as polite as their indigenous English counterparts, whether they are working as sales persons or serving at the tills in supermarkets. They do not tend to say 'thank you' after serving or are not as polite as their English colleagues. This could well be because in their households, although living in England, an old Indian culture might still prevail.

To me personally, when I first went back to India after a gap of nearly 45 years – having lived all these years in one of the politest countries on earth – it was a big culture shock when I found respectable professional people in Delhi, pushing past you in the shops and not saying 'sorry' or 'thank you' or not thanking a waiter or servant after having been served.

During my first visit to my brother's house for dinner, a servant was serving food around the table and when I was served, I said 'thank you' in the middle of a conversation while nobody else thanked him. It surprised everyone sitting there that I had interrupted my conversation to thank an ordinary servant for putting food on my plate. So, that thankfulness and politeness has been injected into me as time has passed. And in India, people find I am overly polite. By contrast, even the well-to-do guests in hotels and smart restaurants rarely say 'thank you' to the waiters.

To me, being thankful is an expression of gratitude. As politeness is an essential virtue that prompts a person to express their gratitude to others, their liberal expression of thankfulness indirectly points towards their politeness. In India, in my opinion, politeness certainly exists but it makes its presence felt through body language and facial expressions rather than words.

A slightly inclined body posture from the waist upwards with folded hands, a downward slant of the neck avoiding direct eye contact and soft speech are good enough to justify one's politeness. Conventional preaching on politeness in India usually cites the example of a tree heavily laden with fruit. As the branches of a tree laden with fruit bow down under the weight of the harvest, a good human being, blessed with wealth and power, is advised to be more polite to others. Though every other person preaches others to be polite in this manner, in common practice, politeness is silently considered as a virtue of the meek.

I was so mystified and overwhelmed by the polite and friendly behaviour of the two policemen I mentioned earlier or by my superiors and bosses in the offices wherever I worked, particularly in the Civil Service. In my experience, civil servants are exceptionally polite to each other, so are Police Officers to each other (after retirement, I worked as a volunteer at a Police Station for about 10 years, so I have observed many examples of this behaviour).

Having lived in England for so long, I have come to feel that merely verbal or physical expression of politeness does not necessarily mean that the person expressing his politeness in either of these manners is really polite from within.

A good number of people adopt the expression of politeness—verbally or by way of body language—in their mannerisms, just to appear polite to others for their individual gain without really being polite in the true sense of the word. Similarly, such other virtues commonly expressed verbally or physically without a spontaneous inner belief may merely be 'tutored virtues' or in other words, 'aesthetic virtues'.

A person who truly believes that every person, or for that matter every other living being, is equal, is spontaneously polite to everyone. This is the true virtue of politeness. Though tutored virtues stand secondary to true virtues, they have their own importance in human life. The English have been tutored in politeness so meticulously by their elders through generations, that over time this tutored virtue has percolated deep into their persona, which has assumed the form of genuine politeness. A very close English friend of mine, Leslie, whenever he meets me, will always ask, 'How is your charming wife? Please give my regards to her.' Once I questioned him why he always asked about my family. He admitted that, from childhood, he was tutored by his mother to be nice and polite to others and ask about the welfare of their families.

The Legendary English Politeness

If the awareness of equality between all living beings leads to genuine politeness, the opposite is also true. Genuine politeness can also awaken a true sense of equality. A total commitment of the majority of the English to democratic principles is the visible outcome of the sense of equality developed over the centuries. The same sense of equality well explains an English person's love for their dog or expressions like 'Don't frighten the horses'.

When I was little, back home, I remember my father telling me an interesting story about the Sikh king, Maharaja Ranjit Singh Ji, who ruled Punjab, Kashmir and Afghanistan during the 17th and 18th centuries. The king was riding through a village accompanied by a few soldiers. Suddenly, a stone hurled by a boy hit him in the eye and he was badly injured. The king asked the boy why he hurled the stone at him. The boy truthfully and respectfully told him that he actually threw the stone at a mango tree, expecting to hit a mango, which he could eat and he did not intend to hurt the king. The king called the boy to come near him and gave him some money to go to the market and buy a load of mangoes for himself. Everyone was surprised by such an unexpected gesture from the king. When asked, the king replied, 'I was impressed by the selflessness of the mango tree. If someone hurls a stone at the tree, it obliges him with a mango. Being a king, I too must act in a noble manner resembling the mango tree.'

Having said that, you cannot help noticing that, even in England, as the younger generations are growing up they are not as polite and grateful as they used to be, but that is a universal problem. The young are in hurry and moving faster today than when I was a boy. They have developed their own way of communicating. They have their own slang even among the well-educated and, of course, the email and the text message have done away with the niceties and formalities of a letter. Second and third generation Indians who have been born and bred in England are English in all their ways. My daughter and granddaughter can hardly speak a word of Hindi. Manners and behaviour among most of the Indian children brought up in England are similar to their English counterparts, because that is seen as their normal culture.

So far as I am concerned, in my early days in England, I noticed that basic politeness was the same wherever I worked in the country. The difference was that in the north politeness is more abrupt—'Ta'—but they are still saying something. Obviously, if you are dressed well, there is more deference whether you are in an office or simply walking down the street.

What I have observed is that with a modicum of politeness you get better service and get noticed. So, we should remember that a little politeness in the English style, goes a long way in England, and possibly anywhere else.

I would not say it is typically English, but I have noticed that repeating someone's name is catching on. Remember the names of people you are introduced to and the people that serve you. Then next time you are in a restaurant or hotel, you can greet them personally. It has a magical effect.

I recall on one occasion I went to the Savoy Hotel in London. It had been some time since my previous visit and a lot of the staff had changed. I went to the Grill Room and asked, 'Is so-and-so still here?' I was told he had left, but that gave the impression to the *maître d'* that I was a regular and so he put me and my guest at a good table and gave us first class service.

It is a very American thing to repeat the name as one is introduced to each other, but as people travel widely nowadays, these habits are being adopted in more and more cultures. When I was at the Ministry of Defence, I went to one American company working on a project in the county of Surrey. I was introduced to the American manager and he immediately responded, 'How do you do, Mr Lall.' It made me feel good that he was recognising me as an individual, as a person.

Remember, one's name is the sweetest thing to an individual— so wrote Dale Carnegie in his classic book *How to win friends and influence people*. But this is very American and perhaps even a little European, although I do admit that it can be very difficult for people to understand foreign names. In addition, nowadays we are also getting a mixed group of people from many different parts of the world. The melting pot has grown much larger and the ingredients are ever more exotic!

The Legendary English Politeness

Quite often I wonder how much of all this courtesy is sincere, particularly in shops and restaurants. In educated private homes in England, I am certain that it is all perfectly genuine, even if said out of habit. A child would be swiftly reprimanded by his or her parents for forgetting their manners. Even in what we might refer to as working class homes, a quick 'Ta' would be expected. In the service industries, such as hotels and restaurants, I feel it is really only a formality, it has no meaning or sincerity. And here is the twist—things seem to have gone full circle. When I go back to India and stay at good hotels, these days I find that this sort of courtesy comes across as being sincere. Yes, of course, the staff in Indian hotels are trained very well. But if they call you 'Sir' they mean 'Sir', whereas if you go to a top class hotel in, say, London or New York or on the continent, their 'Sir' is a dry Sir.

***

There is one other curious aspect of English etiquette which is worth dwelling on for a moment. It is the formal dance of English conversation.

Take for example, the moment someone is introduced to you. In polite society they will say, 'How do you do?' The correct reply is, 'How do you do?' Notice how absolutely no information has been exchanged, but also notice that neither party is the slightest bit interested in how the other is really doing. The last thing they want to know is all about their new acquaintance's health, particularly if they have been ill.

I have to say while this is a typical formal introduction, it also leaves the typical English person in a quandary as to what to say next and so with one leap they will turn to that great English staple of conversation, the weather.

Being naturally reserved, the English will also refrain from asking about someone's job—although this is changing among the younger generation, where there is a preoccupation with money.

It is my feeling that it is just a custom that the English open a conversation with the weather. Then on top of it all, as the saying goes, the English love their privacy and hate to talk about their personal life. That fits very well into my philosophy of life—we are all part of the universal cosmic force. Talking about good things around you is spreading an aura of happiness in that cosmic force.

An English person could live next door to someone for years and not know anything about them. Neighbours are as detached or semi-detached as the houses. Is that polite or impolite or is it nature? Even living in a room in digs you might not know who is living in the same house.

Live your own life, don't get involved—these are the depressing creeds of today and they are sad. They lead to terrible stories about elderly people who have collapsed and died in their anonymous flats and lain undiscovered for days, sometimes even weeks on end.

So have they got it right? Is the stiff upper lip English style, where they abhor any conversation which dwells on personal health, good? There is an apocryphal story of a businessman who arrives late for a board meeting and apologises to his fellow directors for being late, 'Sorry, a spot of bother at home, my dog died this morning!'

The English way is certainly more discreet, to say the least. I am a great believer in trying to spread happiness and by saying you are well, even if you are ill, does keep people happy. If you like, it spreads a good cosmic force. I am all for the English way!

Are the mysteries of English etiquette just that, a mystery? I have found that the English have a certain way of doing things and so long as you make the effort to understand their ways and whims, attempt to adopt their style and mannerisms you will be accepted and welcomed as a professional person wherever you travel in the country.

So by speaking correctly, by behaving as my peers did, by not prying into other people's private affairs unless I was invited, I gradually learned the ropes of English manners and was accepted into my adopted home much more readily than others who stuck to their immigrant culture and remained apart from the mainstream of English society.

Having said that, I am not so naïve as to believe everything in the garden is rosy. We only have to look at the reputation of football supporters abroad or young louts on the London Underground and trains. Discourtesy is an affliction of so many young people today and an increasing lack of respect, whether it is playing their music too loudly on trains or buses, putting their feet on seats or not holding the door open for the person behind you.

The problem is not just among the children but among parents, too. Everyone seems to know their rights but not their responsibilities. It is not PC (Politically Correct) to offer a lady a seat on a bus and some can even take offence if you hold the door open for them, but I am firmly convinced that this is just a blip and if it is not, then there will soon be a backlash against rudeness which is mistaken today for 'cool'.

What I can say for certain is that, in my experience, old fashioned standards still apply in the professional world and in most educated families. I pity those who object to polite conduct, because I have usually found that courtesy and good manners, while costing absolutely nothing, pay handsome dividends in friendships and success.

I can now sit back and observe how much I have learned and how much of the English culture I have absorbed to the extent that I walk and talk and behave as an English person than an Indian. I feel that I have become part of the English culture. I love these expressions now—how do you do, sorry, thank you very much indeed. I do not think I am alone in clinging to these basic courtesies.

And finally, I dare to say that even beggars are exceptionally polite in my England (according to *Reader's Digest*).

Beggar: Sorry to bother you, Sir. Do you happen to have a spare 20 pence?

Me: Sorry mate, I don't.

Beggar: Not to worry—thanks anyway and have a nice day.

And from me, to you—the reader—'Have a pleasant time reading the rest of the book!'

With Deputy Chief Police Commissioner, London

3

Prejudice, the English Way

> Everyone is a prisoner of his own experiences.
> No-one can eliminate prejudices—just recognise them.
>
> Ed Murrow

I had never heard of or felt 'prejudice', in its true sense, before leaving India. It was not something I had ever noticed in my life anywhere earlier as something which could hurt me. However, looking back on my life in India as a youngster, there did exist prejudice against me but I did not notice it or feel it. One example was when I was a child, growing up in Rawalpindi (now in Pakistan). I was looked down upon because I was not a Punjabi and belonged to a family which hailed from the North West Frontier Province and my accent was different. Later on, after partition, when we moved to Bihar and Bengal, I was remarked upon or stamped as non-Bengali, and my family was sometimes accused of being cowards to have run away from Punjab, our homeland.

However, the word prejudice as such was not in my vocabulary. At a later stage in my life in England, I realised that all of us are prejudiced in one way or another, whether knowingly or otherwise.

The word 'prejudice' in its wider sense means a favourable or unfavourable opinion formed in respect of anyone or anything even before experiencing it directly. This means a prejudice is generally formed without authentic knowledge, thought or reason.

The first time I became aware of race, nationality or religion-oriented prejudice was when I started looking for work in London and later on for digs in Manchester. Like every other budding accountant, I sent off job applications everywhere and most of the responses I got were, 'Sorry, nothing available.' I actually took that as correct, because that is exactly what had happened to me in India soon after my graduation.

When I did succeed in getting to the interview stage, for some reason or other I failed to get the job. Eventually, I saw an advertisement from a practice in an accountancy magazine. It turned out to be a firm run by two Jewish partners and I was interviewed by one of them. During the conversation, he asked me if I realised that there was prejudice in the UK against coloureds. Incidentally, it was the first time that I heard the word 'coloured'. I said I had not really noticed any either here or earlier in Austria where I had been living before coming to England. He said it was possibly, because in Austria there were few Indians, but in England there were many. He told me that I would come across prejudice. He also warned me that some of his clients might not like my going to them to do their books, so he would have to take that problem into account when assigning clients to me. Even then, the full significance of what prejudice meant did not really dawn on me. Looking back, I can now appreciate his openness about it because he was Jewish and, of course, Jews had suffered a lot of prejudice before and during the World War. At that moment, I did not know the distinction between the English and the Jews—to me they all looked the same white people.

Happily enough for me, I was offered the job. It was only a small office, with only two or three people. Later, when I got to know them better, one of them told me that when the boss announced that an Indian was about to start work, he had asked if anyone minded. The person also said quite openly that he was not keen on the idea. One of the others admitted that they also felt the same way. If one thinks about that for a moment, it was a remarkable conversation for a person to have in a professional office and perhaps an even more remarkable response. The partner in the firm was clearly taking something of a risk by employing me. Maybe he recognised the problems of oppressed minorities, but it did not stop his employees raising their own small voices of objection against a race of people with whom they would not associate out of choice.

I salute both the partner for his open-mindedness and the employees for admitting to their own prejudice and for allowing themselves to be 'converted' by me over time. Later on, when I started going out on assignments with one of the clerks who was very prejudiced against all non-English, he tried explaining to me that the partners in the firm were Jews. Until then, I had not noticed any difference between the so-called English and Jews. He tried explaining to me that the Jews have dark skin, big noses and so on. Thereafter, I started looking at all English people closely, wondering if they were English or Jew. To tell you the truth, even today I remain confused. Of course, different cultures can adopt different dress codes, so it is often easy to distinguish one group from another.

As time passed, I learnt that some sort of prejudice existed against Catholics also as the office girl quite often talked against them—she said they produced more children so that all England could become a Catholic country. Fifty years later, similar rumours have spread against the Muslims.

The same attitude was there when it came to finding digs and I became familiar with the notices on the windows: 'Room available. Sorry! No Irish, no coloureds, no dogs.' At first I could not understand what they meant by this. It was something I had never seen in India. As soon as they saw my face, they said the room had gone. Later on my wife told me that she had found similar prejudice when she came to London in 1964 as a single girl. She used to work for a social service organisation, so when she was looking for digs she would go along with one of her English colleagues who would knock at the door and ask if a room was available. They would say 'yes' and he would say, 'Well, it's for my friend here.' The owner would then fumble and make some lame excuse to avoid giving the digs to a coloured person.

Looking back on those days, in my odd moments, I sometimes laugh at the whole situation. Thirty years later, when I was running my own successful accountancy practice, included in my staff there were some ten white ladies, including two Jewish ladies. I was letting accommodation to white people—a complete turnaround from my situation thirty years earlier!

At that moment though, it did not strike me as prejudice. I remember on one occasion when I was quite new in Manchester, I was at a telephone kiosk. In those days to make certain calls you had to go through the operator. She could not understand me and I could not understand her and there was someone waiting outside, getting increasingly impatient. Eventually he opened the door and to his credit he helped me. He said to the operator, 'Oh it's some coloured fellow.' Funnily enough, I do not think it was said maliciously. It was just inculcated into the English psyche that coloured people were stupid and could not help themselves. For stupid read 'could not speak English properly'. It is ironic that many English businesses in the 21st century rely heavily on providing customer service through call centres staffed by operators based in the sub-continent, most of whom are educated to degree level.

At a later stage, I realised that neither the operator nor I were really stupid. Though people educated in India knew the English language quite well, they could not speak with the same accent as the English. If I was stupid because I could not understand what the operator said, she was equally stupid, in my opinion, for not understanding what I said in grammatically correct English. Even today, a large number of highly learned people from India can appear to be quite stupid when they speak English in an Indian accent, despite their obvious intelligence, and this can cause chaos in communication.

Generally, a person who cannot understand simple language or fails to convey their thoughts coherently, is termed as 'stupid'. There is nothing wrong in calling a person stupid, but when every coloured person gets generalised as such, it becomes a prejudice.

To tell you the truth, till this day, having lived nearly 60 years in England, I find it difficult to understand a Scottish telephone operator if he or she has got a strong Scottish accent. At the same time I must emphasise that when talking about my early days in Manchester, I am talking about the situation and atmosphere that existed in 1950s and 1960s. Thankfully, things have moved on since then.

So, slowly, it began to sink in that there was some sort of prejudice there. In the beginning it hurt me. Others have suffered the same way. First the Irish and Jews, now in the 21st century the Polish and others from Eastern Europe are being regarded in the same disparaging way. It is the Polish plumbers and builders who are on every building site up and down the country now, 'taking our jobs and our homes'. Back in the late 1950s, it was the minority groups who were the first to accept us. My first flat was with an Irish landlady, the next one with a Jewish lady and then a landlady who was a Catholic—because, remember, the Catholics also faced prejudice back then. Since then, things have changed dramatically. Many laws have passed through all sorts of discrimination, so much so that sometimes these things weigh heavily against the majority communities.

So yes, it did hurt me when I could not get a room, but, generally, I did not notice that such discrimination was widespread and when I did encounter it, I looked at it philosophically. Essentially, we were strangers and we were asking an English family to take a stranger into their home. They were bound to look at us differently, even suspiciously. I like to think I was fairly broad-minded about it and did not do what many others did and try to make a political issue out of it.

I also reflected back on my own experience in Calcutta. I asked myself how many Bengali families would have accepted me being a Punjabi, even though I was a Hindu and belonged to the same country. The answer is, back then, they simply did not accept persons from other states in the country as their outlook, habits and lifestyles differed from their own. A similar attitude of mutual distrust exists to some extent between different communities everywhere. I take it as a part of normal human life. We all have our own prejudices and people have their own circumstances and reasons for being prejudiced. The fact always remained that I was a stranger in their country and it was natural for them to be wary of me. We are all wary of things we do not initially understand and as we become more familiar with them, they become accepted and are treated with total respect.

After qualifying as a chartered accountant in Manchester, I moved to Birmingham and there, for the first time, I felt that there was some sort of real friction. One evening, I was unoccupied. I was walking past the town hall and I noticed there was some political party meeting going on—the Freedom Party. The next day I went to the office and told them that I had been to the meeting and how so many of the speakers had been talking against the Indians and coloureds saying they had TB and were bringing diseases to this country. I had been shocked by their aggressive attitude. My colleagues asked me why on earth I had gone there. I had been naïve I suppose, maybe a little lulled into a false sense of security by the more enlightened atmosphere in a professional office where I had been totally accepted—an equal. Indeed, as time passed, my colleagues were kind enough, even fond enough of me, to invite me to their homes for Christmas dinner.

Among my own professional colleagues, I did not feel any prejudice at all and actually was perhaps even more respected than other English people who had not been to their type of school. They excused my ways of doing things differently. Instead of criticising me, they showed me how it was done in England. They would not have been so indulgent with their fellow English friends.

One firm (KPMG) I worked for had a very fiery tempered senior partner—he was Scottish. It has changed nowadays, but at that time senior partners would shout and call you by your surname. The truth is that he was nasty to everybody, even throwing files at people if he was not happy with their work, but with me he was the kindest person. Other managers would shudder in front of him so they would give some of their jobs to me because they said I could handle him better.

Alright, I probably did one or two jobs well, but I admired his authoritarian manners and the way he took an interest in my work. Perhaps it was because I was used to that sort of behaviour. I remember that my brother, who was quite high up in an American company in India, would shout at his secretaries as a matter of routine for silly mistakes or behaviour, and even at me when I was staying with him. So shouting by this partner did not worry me—rather it endeared me to his bossy ways. When I decided to leave for another job, he called me in to ask why I was going. It amazed my colleagues that the senior partner should bother to enquire why I was leaving.

In that particular office, on a professional level by and large, I was accepted probably because I did not have an English educational background and therefore could not be stereotyped or identified as being out of place. There was one chap who had been to Eton Public School and actually nobody liked him although he and I got on very well. We had prejudice among the indigenous English too, between private school and state school educated people. Outside the work environment, I saw widespread working class prejudice, as if it was normal human behaviour.

Then of course you had in those days Enoch Powell, one of the most respected Members of Parliament and once a Minister in the Conservative Government. The tabloid newspapers picked up on his speeches, totally misunderstanding his message and classical allusions in his so-called Rivers of Blood speech in 1968. Powell was no racist. He once said, *'I have set and will always set my face like flint against making a difference between one citizen of this country and another on grounds of his origin.'* He was a scholar from the age of five, when he learned to read Greek, until the time of his death when he was learning his twelfth language, Hebrew. His predictions about parts of this country becoming almost segregated, with different ethnic groups eventually dominating certain areas to the virtual exclusion of others, have all come to pass. Then, his economic view, later on adopted by Margaret Thatcher and by many developing countries, revolutionised global economies.

The trades unions marched in solidarity with Powell, fearful about their members' jobs. I could understand what they were saying. Instinctively, I do not believe they or the English were racists, but they were worried about foreigners coming over and taking their jobs. And perhaps they had a case. By the end of 2006 it was reported that immigrants were arriving in the UK at the rate of one a minute. At the same time, studies also showed that workers from Eastern Europe—Poland in particular, I recall—were, on balance, a financial asset to the country and were probably directly responsible for keeping inflation down by half a percent. Such are the tensions and dynamics of a modern, open economy.

The 2016 referendum result in the United Kingdom, leading to the process whereby England and the rest of the United Kingdom will leave the European Union (EU), appears to have been based on prejudice against immigration, although it is by no means certain that a departure from the EU will make much difference to the free movement of people. This seems to me to be a classic case of prejudice and reality being very far apart.

Prejudice exists in every country, but there were people in England during the early days of my stay in the country who took advantage of the situation. They made a big show of it. Then of course, later on the Race Relations Act came in, but it is human nature for people to have their likes and dislikes.

Sometimes the discrimination is more subtle, almost invisible. When I was working at the Ministry of Defence, they had Promotion Boards. Three or four times I went to the Board, hoping to land the next graded post. On one occasion I was convinced I would get it, as there were five vacancies for that post and not many qualified candidates. But I did not. I was sure then that there was some sort of a glass ceiling—I was never going to get the job, no matter how well qualified I was.

Then one of the persons in charge of Personnel matters, Human Resources they would call it today, whom I had got to know quite well, took me out to lunch. He said an Indian has got one of the jobs and he told me that his boss, one of the members of the Board at which I was interviewed, had remarked that it was lucky I had not got the promotion otherwise the Board Members might have been accused of being racially prejudiced in favour of Indians and against the English! It was small comfort to me, but at the same time it turned out to be a blessing in disguise. The event made me realise that if I wanted to make serious money, I would have to strike out on my own, which I finally did.

This sort of prejudice, in later years, came to be known as 'institutional racism'. This phrase got coined in the Stephen Lawrence Enquiry report, which said that individual police officers were not racists but there did exist some sort of embedded racism within the police as a whole. (Stephen Lawrence was a black British student from south east London, who was murdered in a racially motivated attack while waiting for a bus on the evening of 22 April 1993.)

Prejudice did exist and still exists in many forms. but before we start throwing stones in glasshouses, we Indians should acknowledge that we have prejudice in our own country too. At one time if you were not of some high caste you would not get the job. If your father had the job before you, you would expect to have it passed on to you. These things happened all the time. Thankfully, there are now laws against discrimination on grounds of caste and the situation in India has improved immensely.

I accept prejudice as part of human nature. If I come across it, I take it in my stride. However, what saddens me most is when ethnic or other minorities—Jews, Hindus or Muslims—criticise the English generally instead of recognising or appreciating their generosity and other good qualities, while overlooking their own prejudices within their communities.

Slowly, I started to realise that in England, having the right necktie helps you. If you have been to the right private school, you will have a greater chance of getting the job. You might call it favouritism since you are still showing a preference for one person over another for reasons other than their qualifications. The Old Boy network, I am certain, is alive and well today as it ever was; if not the same school, then the same club or church or Freemasons' Lodge or other private grouping will do just as well.

Do I disapprove? Probably not. Again, it comes back to human nature, self-preservation and instinct. There are whole districts of London which can be defined entirely by their ethnic groupings; in fact, there are also entire cities which seem to be a magnet for specific ethnic groups.

A major driver in this divisive trend is, undoubtedly, education and it is a worldwide phenomenon. In England everybody is 'literate', but there are very few 'educated', or should I say 'well educated'. I had a good educational background, although I did not have the English politeness and manners. This meant that when I came to work in England, I could not be stereotyped as they would do to a fellow English citizen. Over a period of time, I noticed that the English like to be kind to foreigners, at least among the professional class, who perhaps had some connection with India, their fathers in the army or something similar.

I recall when I was working in Manchester, we had a smaller sub-office in Southport, in which I would occasionally work. There was one chap working there and when he told his mother that they had an Indian working in the office, she asked him to bring me home for dinner. It turned out that her father had been in India and he used to tell very nice stories about his army days there. However, among the working class, I was an intruder, some coloured person coming from a backward country and taking their job.

The media have a lot to answer for in establishing and spreading prejudice, but I do not think it is unfair to say that the upper professional classes read better papers like *The Guardian*, *The Times* and *The Independent*, which take a more balanced attitude and approach to this problem. On the other hand, the tabloids tend to whip up racist-type stories to attract more readers and push up their sales.

There is a danger that one can generalise too much. Attitudes vary considerably up and down the country. Just taking my own experience in Manchester, I think I made friends more easily, people in offices I visited were much more open and friendly, but I did not enjoy my five years in Birmingham. Maybe it is the nature of the city itself—Manchester is a much brighter city. Again, things have changed there, as I am talking about the mid-1960s and since then Birmingham has undergone major investment and is re-defining itself as a cultural and economic centre.

I was, of course, new in the country and there were not many of us around at that time. Reflecting back, I can see that Manchester had a large Jewish and Catholic population, who were kind to Indians, as part of a minority community. Soon after leaving Birmingham, I got married and went to work in Milan, Italy, where I had a brief spell before returning to England, when we settled in London.

So, circumstances at home were also different. My wife already had a circle of friends as she was working in London before our marriage. We bought our own house. We gradually got to know the neighbours and we had a baby. Naturally all the young mothers would get together. By then, what I might call the 'cheap type' of prejudice had virtually disappeared. Yes, it will always be there, but we had become part of the community.

I am not looking back at those days through rose tinted spectacles, though. There was a different sort of prejudice when we were in the process of buying a house. There would be articles in the papers about new Asian people moving into various neighbourhoods, 'taking our houses', perhaps pushing up prices beyond the reach of locals. It is the same everywhere, though, to this day and given time. Once you have moved in, you become part of the neighbourhood yourself, and do not want foreigners next to you. Incidentally, our neighbour was a Police Officer who had a daughter of our daughter's age and we got on very well with one another. He helped us a lot in settling down in our first house.

Socially, today we have more English friends than Indian friends. Even in the early days, when I first started working in Manchester, there were people who were not prejudiced or racist. As I said earlier, one of my colleagues invited me to his house for Christmas and another client and his girlfriend also invited me for Christmas. These people respected Indian culture and understood it.

Have attitudes changed in the early part of the 21st century? The honest answer is, it probably depends where you live and work. The people we go out with are all professional people, many of whom have travelled and lived abroad, including India. For example, the Chief Executive of London City Airport, Richard Gooding, had spent two years in the Indian sub-continent when he was working for British Airways. We became very good friends via the Chamber of Commerce of which he was the President while I was a Chair Person. Socially, we went out quite often. My wife and I were the only Indians invited to his 60th birthday party.

Similarly, the Chief Executive of Newham Council, Dave Burbage, and his wife Rita, were very sociable with us. We went to each other's houses. My boss, Eric Shipton, at the Ministry of Defence, was very kind and we remained friends for a long time after my leaving and his retirement, until his death at the age of 92. Even one bank manager, Ron Thomas, and his wife, got on so well with us they would come to our house and we would get invited to their house. At one stage, he did remark that I was the only customer whom he had ever invited to his house.

So, here is an Indian who is being invited to a bank manager's house in preference to his English customers. This proves the point that at the human level, we all can live in harmony. On the other hand, my wife, who worked in social services and then started working as a school teacher after the birth of our child, was exposed to more abusive behaviour. Some of the mothers at the school were nasty to her. In some of the poorer, deprived areas where conditions are tough for families and schools alike, that attitude has probably not changed much.

I deal with the whole question of class elsewhere in the book, but this ignorant attitude of racial prejudice probably comes down to class. The upper classes understand and respect foreigners and understand their cultures as they are well read and travelled, but the lower classes not only despise foreigners but also their own people if they are not from the same background, because that mentality exists in their minds. It is a 'them' and 'us' attitude.

This reminds me of my earlier days in India when I was young. Train travel was an ordeal in those days. There used to be no reservations on the train, especially in third class. During vacations, when I travelled to visit members of my family, usually the compartments were packed with passengers and their luggage, with people crouching on the seats, squatting on the floor, as well as perching on the luggage racks. At every station, whereas a few passengers alighted from the train, at least an equal or even larger number would board it. If the passengers on the platform were eager and anxious to enter the compartment, the passengers inside were all the more anxious not to let them enter in order to avoid additional crowding inside. This caused a great tussle between the 'insiders' and the 'outsiders'. Ultimately, a lucky few could enter the compartment and a few unlucky ones could not. After an initial lull for some moments, the 'intruder' would exchange a few smiles and slowly make friends with others by asking their names, what they did, how well they were doing and so on. By the time the train reached the next station, this 'intruder' would become an accepted 'insider' and then enthusiastically join others in their struggle to obstruct the 'outsiders' from the platform from entering the compartment. This is why I do not look at this attitude of 'them' and 'us' as prejudice, but consider it more as human nature and as an individual concern for protecting one's comfort and security.

Coming back to the class culture, it is not my intention to say that people from the higher class are necessarily good people or those belonging to the lower class are bad. After all, people are people and they could be good or bad irrespective of their class, culture, education and relative prosperity. Notwithstanding whether they are good or bad, the people from a higher class are definitely better informed, more widely travelled and enjoy wider interaction with different people and cultures. As I said earlier, if the lack of adequate knowledge is responsible for forming prejudices, a better informed person is naturally well equipped in rising above them.

This reminds me of a wonderful couplet from Mirza Ghalib, the great 19th century Urdu poet from India. In this couplet, the poet invokes mercury to coat a sheet of glass so that it becomes a mirror and produces multiple images so that our narrow vision widens enough due to multiple imaging, leading to better understanding of truth. If a human mind resembles a clear sheet of glass, experience and wisdom act as the coating of mercuric oxide. Naturally, knowledge and experience facilitate the human mind in creating multiple images of situations and events and ultimately help it rise above the prejudices caused by narrow-mindedness.

I suppose you cannot change human nature. It is human nature to be prejudiced. Wherever I have come up against prejudice or intolerance—such as some pub where they did not want to serve me a drink—I would just leave, with no ill feeling.

It is human nature for one to feel superior to someone else and that is a sort of prejudice. A story goes that Gandhiji was walking with an English clergyman on the pavement of a street in South Africa. Some young people passed by on the other side of the street and shouted 'nigger boy'. Gandhi remarked to the clergyman, 'How strange it is! We all are human beings but one human being feels or thinks that he is superior to another because of his education or upbringing or the colour of his skin.' When you are successful, it does not matter so much. Successful people have a certain aura about them which always demands respect and actually some people have a natural aura which marks them out from an early age as individuals who are destined to make an impact.

The important point is that I came across and still come across prejudice during my life here in England, but I never got bogged down by it nor allowed it to make me bitter. Bitterness is self-destructive, whereas love creates and generates more love.

Enoch Powell was just saying what he thought and he was giving a warning that too much immigration to this country would have a negative effect. He was right. In fact, I was a great admirer of Enoch Powell and his intellect. Incidentally, he had some good economic ideas as a staunch monetarist and believer in market forces—something all other political parties eventually came to believe in. Baroness Thatcher, when she was the Prime Minister, claimed her monetarist ideas stemmed from his ideas, to which he is reported to have replied, 'A pity she didn't understand them.' Enoch Powell was very good in using metaphors such as 'Rivers of Blood'. On his economic views, he quite often used to say, 'Why are we treating the pound sterling as a sacred cow? Let it float in the open market.' That is what has been done in the UK and other countries under the principles of liberalisation and the countries have progressed economically and otherwise due to this.

My elder brother used to travel a lot to Russia, America and Europe, and quite often he would write back to me at home saying, 'People are the same everywhere. It is just the politicians who try to make look us different and find the differences.' A mother and her child are the same everywhere. She will cling tightly to her baby to protect her child the same way all over the world.

In view of all this, can we have an open mind? If we try to get away from this feeling of belonging, I think the world would be a better place. I think the most prejudiced people are those who think they are oppressed. I find the Scots, Irish, Welsh, Catholics, Jews and now Hindus, Sikhs and Muslims are like that because they all feel oppressed by the English. However, while the English also have this strong sense of belonging, they also exhibit an open minded attitude towards others. Not only can they accept other cultures but they can also adopt other cultures. They are prepared to give everyone an opportunity.

England is the least narrow minded of all the countries, in my opinion, having lived in India, Austria and Italy. England my love, is just great!

Well this is how I see it, being fully aware that this individual point of view could also be fairly classified as a prejudice!

4

The English Reserve

Man does not strive for pleasure—only the Englishman does.

Friedrich Wilhelm Nietzsche

I wonder, is the famous English reserve is a myth when it comes to the delicate question of sex? There is no question that true English people are reserved and I believe that simply stems from not wanting to impose themselves on other people, being discreet, polite, holding back where others might dive in.

Now, of course, I can only speak of people of a certain age—teenagers and students are largely a law unto themselves in the 21st century—but even among them, I suspect the natural born English man or woman is still the quietest one in the group.

The phrase 'still waters run deep' springs to mind here, but I am sure at times the waters are so still that you have to go down to the very deepest fathoms to find any flow at all.

When I first arrived in England, there was no doubt that the average English people I came across in business and socially were very reserved characters. In part, that may have been because they were dealing with a foreigner, but I found that most men were more comfortable in the company of other men and became unsettled when women were introduced the 'lads together' syndrome which I am quite certain persists even today.

The problem may be due to schooling. Mixed schools in the UK are commonplace, but single sex schools are equally commonplace in the private sector. What I find peculiar is that regardless of the type of education an English male has received, he will still instinctively feel more comfortable with other males, certainly into his late teens. Even after that, many will look forward to their boys-only days out.

Compare that with, say, the French who will certainly have had a mixed-sex education whether it was private or public. A French man will always have socialised with girls and will feel completely relaxed in their company. The same, I suspect, applies to Italians and Spanish; the interesting point about Italy and Spain is that they are matriarchal societies. Now the English believe they are a patriarchal society, but I think that women in fact hold the upper hand.

I offer absolutely no scientific reasoning for this, but it probably comes back to the fear of women; English men do not really understand how women work, because the English males are not touchy-feely; most do not have a feminine bone in their bodies. The Asians are quite likely to touch someone's arm when they are talking or to make a point; the English would never dream of intruding into someone's personal space in that manner. They will step further and further back from anyone talking to them if they get too close. They simply feel uncomfortable with physical proximity.

One of the funniest moments in English public life was when Margaret Thatcher became the leader of the Conservative Party and then the Prime Minister. In the House of Commons, she was in her famous blue outfits surrounded by a sea of grey suits. The boys around her were clearly terrified of her—on both sides of the House. Not only was she female, but she also had a better grasp of all departments than any of her Ministers and all of the Opposition. She was often regarded by commentators as 'the best man' in the Cabinet. Similar feelings were expressed about Indira Gandhi - the only woman Prime Minister of India - that she also was 'the only man' in her Cabinet.

So if the English reserve is a given, is it a disability or an asset? I think there is a definite charm about it. An English tycoon with a lot of wealth would dress down, modestly, to the point of dilapidation. Some aristocrats with rolling acres and stately homes have often been mistaken for the gardener as they wander around their estates in old trousers and jumpers. That is self-confidence. They are comfortable with who they are, they have nothing to prove and would be too embarrassed to draw attention to themselves in any way.

There is a danger that such reserve can be mistaken for arrogance. Nothing could be further from the truth, indeed in all probability the reserved behaviour is to cover up what can be a crippling shyness. It is a wonder that the true English race has not died out. For that, one has probably got to thank the English ladies who, with the typical perspicacity of their sex, have managed to see through the camouflage surrounding the timid creature standing in the corner wishing the party would come to an end as quickly as possible, and dragged him on to the dance-floor and then, in time, to a church, only for them to live happily ever after. There is many a successful English businessman who has a wife in the background to thank.

So what about sex? Instinctively, every English male will squirm uncomfortably at the very mention of the word, or blush uncontrollably. But just a moment, is this all pretence? The Victorians were so prudish that they covered their pianos with decorative cloths so they hung down, covering the legs. Yet behind closed doors, the Victorians were anything but prudish. Indeed, Queen Victoria herself had nine children.

It was common practice in Victorian times for people to avoid expressions of affection in letters. Instead, they used a type of code and explicit erotica was everywhere—even Queen Victoria herself liked to draw male nudes.

Generally, though, the Victorians considered man as full of energy who had to go out and forage, while the woman was the passive partner who had to conserve what little energy she had to endure menstruation (considered a form of mental instability) and give birth.

We have moved on from there, but how is the English male coping today? Is he still striving for pleasure or is it beginning to come more naturally to him? I suspect he is still struggling. An English author could never have written the Karma Sutra—an Italian maybe, a French author possibly, but never an English one.

Consider for a moment how the classic English male seeks his fun—dare I say pleasure. There is an almost overwhelming urge to join a club. In days gone, by many of these clubs were all-male preserves. Why? Because the true English male felt comfortable in cosy leather armchairs, eating food he could recognise (often from his school days) and when there was absolutely no chance of encountering anyone of the female variety. In short, he felt safe at the club. There is a splendid book by Adam Clapham called *Beware Falling Coconuts: Perspectives of India by a BBC Producer* which has some glorious insights into English club life.

Clubland, in the 21st century, is a rather different affair—fast, furious and glamorous for those with the energy and deep enough pockets. There is nothing reserved about these glittering stars of the modern celebrity circuit, but theirs is a fairly transient life—both of the club and stardom. Fashions change and the pop and film star entourage quickly tires of one venue and moves on to the next hot spot. However, these are the people of the gossip columns, not every day life, and serve only to highlight the more traditional English male.

This, though, should not all be about the male of the species. How has the English female changed? In a word, greatly. The stereotype 'quiet English rose' who dutifully followed in her husband's footsteps is no more. Today she may well be a high-flying business leader in her own right. She certainly has a point of view and is not hesitant to express it. Much depends as ever on one's position in life; hard pressed, working class Mums, struggling to keep the family together, as well as trying to hold down a job to supplement their husband's income, may well have a point of view and if they have the chance, they will express it. Further up the ladder, in a curious way, wives may not need to work and therefore sometimes may feel a little more subservient, in the sense that they are entirely reliant on their husband.

Now I should actually mention 'partners' and not just wives. Either out of self-confidence or some sort of sense of rebellion or because they do not believe in it, many couples—an increasing number—do not bother getting married. Reserve in this instance seems to have disappeared altogether.

It all seems a long way from the Victorians, but I believe the basic natural instinct of the English is to be reserved in all matters and that includes relationships with the opposite sex. It stems from their innate sense of politeness and complete antipathy towards all things pushy or ostentatious, including themselves. The young English male of today certainly spends more time getting ready to go out, preparing his hair, bathing himself in body lotions and selecting the right clothes. In all probability, a young teenage boy today will spend longer getting ready to go out of an evening than his mother. His father will leave it to the last minute, quickly shave, push a comb through his hair and be ready.

The England I first arrived in in the fifties has changed in so many ways and yet the essentials I am convinced remain the same, ingrained like a message in the stick of rock which used to be popular back then. I think there is a slight trend to loosen up, as they say, but it does not come naturally to an English male to let his hair down. He will certainly do so at university, partying into the small hours, but then he will revert to type, at least in public.

Behind closed doors—like the Victorians—there may well be a different story to tell. From time to time we get headlines about Government Ministers or other well-known figures caught *in flagrante*, usually by someone cashing in on a few moments of passion. There is nothing so foolish as a man when it comes to sex, particularly when age is creeping on. The passion is still there, regardless of nationality, but judgement can be clouded in the face of young temptation.

Perhaps that is why men sought sanctuary in their clubs. They could boast of past conquests, safe in the knowledge that there was no female to laugh at them and, equally, no female to lead them astray. Nowadays Clubland is altogether more exciting and dangerous. If you are young enough, it seems there are no restrictions. The same story is true in India. There is a younger, wealthier generation, bent on partying and spending their newly earned wealth. Rich rewards have come quickly the world over and with those rewards has come enormous confidence, perhaps even transcending natural timidity.

So does the English male have to strive for his pleasure? I would put it this way—he probably has to work a little harder at it than his Continental cousins. I do not know whether this simply comes down to natural rhythm—something no English person would claim as a national characteristic—or whether reserve is so much part of the English character that they have to work harder than most at being an outgoing, party animal. Faced with a room of people he had never seen in his life, would an English man feel happy about diving in, introducing himself to complete strangers and having a good time? Unlikely. But the educated English would be able to do it, or at least go through the motions because of upbringing and a self-confidence which comes of being English. Strange as it may sound, the very accident of birth of being English seems to bestow both a blessing and a curse—the blessing is what comes from being born English, enormous determination and confidence that comes from a tiny nation which is respected the world over, and the curse, or charm depending on your point of view, of English diffidence, reserve. It is surely the mark of the English that they will not get flustered by any challenge or indeed any compliment.

A young English male will probably be embarrassed by a flirtatious girl at a party, not knowing where to put himself; at once delighted by the attention but lacking the prematurely suave sophistication of, say, his best friend from school who happens to be French and quickly whisks the girl onto the dance floor. The difference? The French friend will most likely forget about the girl by the end of the evening, while the Englishman will think about her for weeks to come and one day they will meet again accidentally and may even get married!

Is this the English reserve that I love so much?

5

The Meaning of English Family Life

> All happy families resemble each other,
> each unhappy family is unhappy in its own way.
>
> Anna Karenina, Leo Tolstoy

Over my years in England, I have seen many changes in the family way of life. It looks as if a revolution has taken over the society in England, compared to 60 years or so ago when I first arrived here. I then compared it with India when I returned after 45 years. India has changed in this respect but it has not taken on the dimension of a revolution as in England.

I had great disbelief or shock observing many things 60 years ago in England when I first arrived here. For example, English men and women often kiss each other in public. Even today in India, kissing in public is deemed by many to be inappropriate and not permissible, although underneath it all, Indian society, particularly urban society, has changed a lot. In England, women are much freer now. Their drinking habits, dress code and other aspects of their lives have changed with the times. At the same time, I would say that basic family structures are still there. I come across quite a few young people who still seem to have respect for their parents. No family unit is perfect and the usual family arguments and disputes are all there, but despite everything, there is very little talk in terms of a breakdown of family structures.

I see that the family way of life is today almost a contradiction in terms. Apart from solidarity in the present day family bonds, the sanctity of the family structure is also under threat. Here in England, the number of people getting married is on the decline, according to the statistics. Two questions immediately suggest themselves—why is this happening, and is it peculiar to my England? The latter question is easier to answer. The phenomenon is not restricted to England alone and we can see a similar trend of gradually weakening family bonds all over the world.

In finding the answer to the first question, we may find many different reasons for such a situation, depending upon the varying socio-economic conditions. However, the most important reason could be attributed to the ever-changing needs and concepts of human happiness. I can see that the amazing achievements the human race has recorded in the fields of science, industry, agriculture and commerce over the past few centuries have a strong influence over the change in human needs and concepts of happiness. This global phenomenon has certainly influenced our lifestyle and hence the family way of life in England as well as in other countries.

This issue is not as simple as it may look outwardly and it needs much deeper thinking into the reasons that created the family system in the first place. The Universe, encompassing Nature and all living beings within its fold, consists of a perpetually interdependent support system and the growth and prosperity of its elements are also interdependent. If Nature grows, life grows and if life grows, Nature grows. Like human beings, Nature does not consider growth in terms of money and personal property. Growth and continuity of all living species including plant life means the growth and continuity of Nature.

That is why Nature has provided all living beings with a compulsive urge for regeneration to ensure that the multiplication of all species continues ceaselessly. This compulsive urge for regeneration lures an otherwise solitary being into taking his or her first step towards starting a family. With this first step, the individual initially integrates with another individual of the opposite sex as a partner and as a result they produce a child. In this process both the partners develop a sense of belonging towards each other as well as their child and it is this very sense of belonging that creates love between all the three.

One must not forget that each of the two partners needed their own sets of parents who brought them into the world, causing a sense of belonging between them, too. A sense of belonging causes the bond of love. Every being desires to live forever, which in turn expresses itself in the form of love for self. Everyone who loves his/her self also naturally loves everything that belongs to him/her because of a 'me' and 'mine' relationship between them. It is due to this sense of belonging that mothers and fathers love their children and brothers and sisters love one another and their parents, causing a bond of love between them and causing them to stick together as one family.

In days gone by, you could have seen similarities between the Indian and English family and home structures. Both would have been used to large families, both would have seen more than two generations living under one roof. The grandparents would have helped care for the children, passing on traditions as well as standards, while the parents were otherwise occupied.

The word 'commitment' is an alien word for the new generation as it consists of too much of discipline, obligation, having to do something for someone else, all of which are unpopular. Today everything is 'I'. The word 'we' suggests having to take someone else's point of view into consideration.

We may blame the young by saying that today they are in a rush to leave home and do their own thing; they are too impatient to cope with granny's funny ways and Mum and Dad of course do not understand them. So as quickly as possible they fly the nest. The old concept of owing a debt to parents is alien to current English culture. Here the Welfare State is supposed to look after you from cradle to grave. But love is always reciprocal; we must sow love first to harvest love in the future.

The main problem of parents today is that they are blindly running after money and enjoying their lives in any way possible.

No one seems to have any spare time. Everyone is busy being busy. No one really can blame them for this attitude as this has become the order of the day. Life has become so much faster, tougher and competitive today that everyone has to work more and more for their survival. Even socialising today means more of contacts and business rather than pleasure.

Working hours in city offices are getting longer and more full of pressure because mortgage payments are high or school fees are rocketing. The rest of the time parents are off enjoying themselves at clubs, meeting their friends or going shopping. Children spend their time during the day at school and with their baby sitter in the evening. When they wake up to go to school, their father is asleep and when they go to bed, their parents are away. Many children grow up in boarding schools and meet their parents during vacations only. When the parents have no time to spend with their children, they definitely have no time to look after their own parents, too. How can such parents expect their children to love them only because they could afford to send them to the most lavish boarding school? No doubt such children would never hesitate to leave their parents at the earliest opportunity and live in their own way because their parents failed to create a bond of love in the family.

What I have discussed above is a situation not restricted to England alone but is also applicable to urban life in many countries. Due to skyrocketing land prices, living accommodation is getting costlier day by day, pushing more and more people towards smaller flats and ultimately breaking up large families into nuclear family units. In the nuclear structure of flat dwelling, there is barely room for the basic family. But it is not only a question of space.

Bombay (now called Mumbai) is famous for its Chawls. A Chawl is a building four to five storeys high with twelve or even more two-room tenements on each floor with a common wall between the two, all served by a central staircase. There are common toilets for the residents at two extreme ends of the building. The two rooms in each tenement are arranged one behind the other and they serve as sitting room, bedroom, kitchen and dining room. One can see up to three generations living together in these two-room tenements of a Chawl, so the traditional family unit is still in evidence. I think that what really matters is the space a person carries in his heart rather than the size of a flat.

Yes, the space in one's heart can do wonders, but it is the bond of love that creates such a space in the hearts of every family member. When this inner accommodation does not exist anything can happen between the persons in even close relationships.

Now in many Indian households in the UK, the grandparents are still around but it is interesting to note that changes of attitude can be detected in India. A recent report from Delhi spoke of the shocking and growing disregard for the elderly. It appears that some upwardly mobile young Indians were persuading their parents to sell the family home to get something bigger so they could all live more comfortably together, only quite literally to throw their parents onto the street or abandon them in an old age home.

The worst story of all was of one very frail mother who was actually taken to a crematorium, but was saved when one of the staff noticed her moving. Help the Aged, a UK charity, was quoted as saying: 'Children want their father's property but not the father.' Admittedly such horror stories are probably rare but they point to one conclusion: the young believe they can do without the support of older generations; they do not see the need to draw on their experience and wisdom.

Thinking back a bit, in earlier times, life revolved round the home, then the village, town or city. Most children used to get absorbed within the traditional family enterprise, be it agriculture or any other trade. Work was local and one's future life was probably local, too. In such circumstances, the extended family environment would have been relatively easy to maintain. Times have changed now and you cannot put the genie back in the bottle. We are now world citizens, often with international careers. It is common for people to have two homes in two different countries. There is not much room for the grandparents in such arrangements.

When I first came to England, I was, of course, lonely and the welcome I received from virtual strangers, although work colleagues, was overwhelming. Everyone needs a sense of belonging. At the same time, I was shocked to hear colleagues talking disrespectfully about their father or mother, husband or wife as 'my old man' or 'old woman'.

I suspect, in time, people will come to regret the nuclear approach where granny and grandpa are despatched to an old people's home at the earliest opportunity. In England, caring for the elderly is big business. Again, in common with many parts of the world, the population is ageing, there is a pension crisis racing towards us, as fewer and fewer workers have to support an increasing numbers of pensioners.

For many elderly people left alone by their own family, their fellow 'inmates' in their old people's home become their new family. The initial enthusiasm for real family members to visit gradually wanes or the visits themselves become less frequent. In time their days are spent either staring out of a window or just straight ahead in the common room, waiting for the next meal until it is time to go to watch their favourite TV programme or just to go to bed once more.

Of course, for every rule there is an exception and there is an army of carers—many unpaid family members—who do an amazing job. It is not uncommon for young people to have to look after their ailing parents, then rush off to school having got their siblings ready, pick up some shopping on the way home and then get their parents ready for bed. Now, in a larger family set up this would not be a problem, but I wonder if things have gone too far?

I feel I should touch on arranged marriages in this context, even though I am living in England like so many of my fellow countrymen and women from India. I do not intend to criticise or comment one way or another on the practice which is just as prevalent in the UK among Indians as it is at home. I use the word 'arranged' in a fairly broad sense. Parents will obviously want the best for their daughters or sons and will contrive to make sure they meet a 'nice' boy or a 'decent' girl. It does not always work out and in civilised families all one can do is move on. There are occasional horror stories where revenge attacks occur against the boy and girl, but on the whole this is rare in the UK.

The English approach to courtship and marriage is pretty loose. You might say the English enjoy a free-style type of attitude. Take the university for example, where young men and women are thrown together, cheek by jowl, and left to get on with it. That can be quite a daunting experience, say, for a young Indian girl who in all probability went to local day schools and, of course, was home every night. Suddenly, she is faced with the prospect of Halls of Residence if she does not get into a university close by. Alcohol and constant parties are reputedly the order of the day—it is quite a challenge to everything to which she may have been accustomed. Her parents will look on in absolute horror.

By contrast, her English fellow students may have been to boarding schools all their lives and be perfectly at ease with communal living or may have gone to local day schools but without the strict controls of a traditional Indian home.

For most university students, they are making friends for life and in many cases will be meeting their future partners. After Halls they will be finding their own flats, no doubt crammed with other students, but already the concept of living away from home, fending for themselves has begun.

Love and marriage go together like a horse and carriage, so the song goes but, alas, divorce is also close behind. I think this comes back to commitment. The traditional marriage vows in England speak of marriage as being 'for better or for worse', but today it seems it is just for better, just for the good times!

Can you imagine anything so cold and calculating, so certain to spread distrust as a pre-nuptial agreement? This document is really just a cynical reflection of our times; *yes I would like to marry you but at the back of my mind I am wondering if you are really only interested in my family fortune or my dowry and for that reason, for that element of doubt, I am protecting myself and my money from any possible dishonest or dishonourable thought that might be in your mind.* Quite a lot to say as you get down on bended knees and ask your sweetheart to spend the rest of their life with you!

Of course, the role in marriage among English couples differs from the traditional one. In the earlier times, the husband worked and the wife stayed at home and ran the domestic side of the household. In the current English home, the same may apply, but more likely it is on a more equal footing. Both partners will have their say in all decisions from decorating the house, to where to send the children to school—in fact, every element of running the family as opposed to just running the home. In all probability, both partners will be out to work; in some cases the wife may be the bigger earner, she may not even want to have children.

Modern married life is a complicated and troubled affair and it would be a brave person who would claim to have all the answers, or any of the answers, but one thing is certain—for a marriage to survive the tensions and the temptations, it requires work and, of course, commitment.

The irony is that there is a growing trend to trace our ancestors, to look back in time to where the family has come from and how it developed. There is a certain pride in being able to identify relatives as far back as possible. It does not matter if an ancestor was noble or a criminal, the important point is being able to trace one's roots. But if things persist as they are, family trees of the future will be fragmented affairs and a drafting nightmare for genealogists.

I am an English citizen and a product of a world where there is no longer any need to cling to one village, town or even country. I left my country of birth because I did not feel there were opportunities for me there and I left behind my family members. My brother had always lived a life of his own, marrying a girl outside our family structure who was very American-orientated having been to an American Public School in Missouri. You might say we are a classic disjointed family. I settled in England, a country which adopted me and gave me an opportunity to build a life, and it became my new home and a place to bring up my family. I never have any doubts about the wisdom of my decision to leave India because it worked for me in so many ways, but it would also be true to say that I do not have the support of the extended family set up of old.

So what have we achieved here in England? Which system is better? The latest UNICEF report puts England at the bottom of a league table of 21 industrialised countries for its care of children.

The report looked at a number of indicators, including family, and put the blame in a large part on the 'dog eat dog' society. Sweden is somewhere near the top and yet Sweden has one of the highest suicide rates in the world. So what is the answer? Will it all reverse as John Steinbeck wrote in *Travels with Charley*?

'And I am sure that, as all pendulums reverse their swing, so eventually will the swollen cities rupture like dehiscent wombs and disperse their children back to the countryside. This prophecy is underwritten by the tendency of the rich to do this already. Where the rich lead, the poor will follow, or try to.'

It may be too late for that as property prices rocket high in the country, but the question is, will the pendulum swing back? Will true family life appeal? Or what will it take to restore the attractions of an extended family?

How easy is it to bring up a family in England as compared with other countries? In my experience, it has been remarkably straightforward. In England there is no criticism when things go wrong, there is no great cloud or accusations of dishonouring the family. Everyone is struggling and managing along as best they can, making do with the cards they have been dealt. A broken home, as they are euphemistically called, is regrettably so commonplace that they are almost the norm. But maybe the tide is turning.

The latest statistics show divorce rates in England (and Wales) have fallen to their lowest in five years—apparently couples are more willing to make a go of it because of the high emotional and financial cost of divorce and the effect it has on the children. But it seems that if you do re-marry, you do not feel the same compunction about breaking up as the number of people divorcing after remarrying has nearly doubled in the past 25 years to a fifth of all divorces. And, of course, fewer and fewer people are turning to wedlock. They are just living together.

So family life—do we cling to it and preserve it? Surely we must, the pendulum will indeed swing back, it always does and then there will be a reckoning. Happy are the homes where there is room for the older generations to pass on their knowledge and lend a helping hand, or where their experience encourages them to say, 'No'. You are the judge—England my love.

6

An Englishman's Home Is His Castle

Home is where the heart is and hence a moveable feast.

Angela Carter

England is my home and has been my home for nearly 60 years, but is there an invisible thread pulling at the heart strings of people like me who have left the land of their birth?

I can only speak for myself and say that while there is a history, there is no longer a tie with the land of my birth. For practically 45 years, I did not visit India. My contacts with my brothers and sisters were basically intermittent correspondence or meeting them if they happened to visit England.

After my retirement, I wrote a couple of books, one of which was published and launched in India by the British High Commissioner. It was then that I started going back to India two to three times a year for two weeks at a time. During my visits, I receive a special sort of respect as a successful Indian returning from abroad. I stay in top class hotels, travel around in chauffeur-driven Mercedes or Jaguars and make speeches at various seminars, being interviewed by press reporters and TV channels. This all gives me a sort of ego satisfaction in my retirement, particularly bearing in mind that some 60 years ago, I walked or biked on those Delhi roads as a lonely young man without any future to look forward to.

Although I have been back to India in my later years for short visits, I do not seem to have any intention to return and spend the remaining years of my life there. I have moved on and become accustomed to a different way of life. I know there are many who leave their native lands, travel extensively but in the end return home. When I was running my accountancy practice, I had a number of Muslim clients who had lived most of their lives in England but at the end their bodies had been sent to their native villages to be buried there. Among the devout Hindus, they wanted their ashes to be scattered in the Holy Ganges and there are many other similar examples of this type of wish. In a way it is natural but, in my opinion, it is a shallow type of sensitivity. The whole world is one's home. To me, England, particularly East London, has become my home, having started and run my business around here for more than 40 years. Whenever I go away, even for holidays, I miss my own house. I miss my English friends. Home is there where you want to be and not where your roots are!

If you really feel the need, it is possible to live entirely with people from your own country of origin in a different land. There are Indian, Arab and Chinese neighbourhoods the world over and for every other nationality in between. You can eat your national dishes, pray in your national church, mosque or temple (although there are restrictions in some Muslim and Communist countries) and even speak your own national tongue from morning till night while watching satellite broadcasts of your favourite local soap operas. But that was never my way.

The word 'home' over and above its universally accepted meaning, defines itself in a number of ways. The Vedas are texts from ancient India. Written in Vedic Sanskrit, the texts represent the oldest forms of Sanskrit literature and the oldest scriptures of Hinduism. In Vedic terms, the soul dwells within a physical body and from there, experiences the external world. However, this basic home, a united body and mind complex, builds a structure with walls and a roof for its shelter and protection and calls it a 'home'. A cluster of such individual homes gets identified as a village and, finally, as a home for every individual person.

Migrant labourers from the economically deprived area spread all over the country, where they work and live for years. They invariably refer to their present dwelling place as a temporary residence, and refer to their village and state as their home. All individual homes gradually integrate into a wider term as a village, state and a country. Even the countries finally integrate into one world. Saints from India, with this wider perspective, identify the entire world as one family, 'For those who live and think beyond self, the entire earth is one family, one home.' In this order, the entire universe is finally seen as a home.

Though I call England my home in a wider sense, I have discussed here 'home' in its different forms, too. All of us know the difference between what we call a 'house' or a 'home'. It is the sense of belonging that makes the real difference. The sense of belonging always carries two aspects with it, one being objective and the other subjective. As long as a person claims a house as belonging to them, it only remains a material object made of bricks and mortar. A house becomes a home for someone who is attached to it subjectively and, therefore, belongs to it. With this specific sense of belonging at the subjective level, I call England my home as I very strongly feel that I belong here.

I would urge anyone thinking of emigrating to a new land to at least explore and understand the local ways. I would go further and advise them to try and adopt local customs and definitely learn the local language. Why bother living in England if you have no interest in the English and their customs? Why go to Rome if you hate pasta? In fact, in England it is now a requirement to have some mastery of English to live permanently here.

Isolationism, for that is what it amounts to, was never an option for me and I dived into English culture wholeheartedly. My motto has always been to identify with the local ways and I would say that it has stood me in good stead wherever I have lived. Even in India, as a young man, when I was uprooted and had to live in the states of Bihar and West Bengal, I adopted the customs of those states (so much so that I even learnt the Bengali language) and therefore was accepted in those societies.

So what does home life mean in England? Like so much that one can discover here, it has everything from pomp to poverty and I will try and touch on a few of these aspects.

Let us start at the bottom. There was a wonderful song performed by Flanagan and Allen called *Underneath the Arches* (originally written in 1927), supposedly about two old tramps whose home was beneath railway arches in London, possibly next to Charing Cross station. Apart from being a favourite song of the time, arches remain a home for many down and out individuals today. Life on the road, sleeping in cardboard boxes or trying to capture the heat from a ventilation shaft of the Savoy Hotel is a reality for many. I do know that some would not live any other way, enjoying the freedom such a precarious existence gives them, living off the discards of other people. Some well-to-do families' children will go all the way to India or Nepal to have a taste of this type of life. For most, it is usually as a result of tragic circumstances, with as many different reasons for their situation as there are people. Sadly, there is an increasing number of young people living rough. Many are attracted to the bright city lights but are all too quickly caught up in drugs and prostitution. It happens the world over, people living in the lowest levels of the society. In fact, in England, allowances are made for homeless people when it comes to counting the numbers of citizens in the Census, which takes place every ten years. If a person sleeps regularly in a particular shop doorway or railway arch, then they are included in the Census figures.

Most of us would blame the curse of poverty for such a precarious lifestyle, but we also know that poverty may not be the only reason. A few years ago the hippie culture spread over the entire world, like religion. Young people belonging to both the 'haves' and 'have nots' classes succumbed to the allure of a vagabond life which hippies supposedly enjoyed. Most human beings secretly nurture a rebel hidden somewhere within their persona. What unknown external reasons may provoke this original spark of rebellion, we know not and yet we all have definitely seen the results.

Mirza Ghalib, one of the most popular 19th century poets from India, expressed a similar desire for freedom from all the worldly affairs in one of his poems. The message of that poem can be expressed in English as:

May I go and live somewhere,
Where there is none,
Neither to share my feelings,
Nor understand my tongue.

May I make a home where,
There are no doors, no walls,
Neither friends, nor guards.

May I fall sick but,
Nurse there be none and
If I die, a mourner
There be none.

Climbing up the social and economic ladder, England is not alone in having tower blocks where life for some is scarcely better than that of vagabonds. Crime and drugs are never far away and grinding poverty makes it difficult for individuals and families to cope. The police admit that there are some neighbourhoods like this where there are no patrols and a sort of lawlessness prevails—particularly at night. The knife-culture dominates and life is cheap. These tower blocks were built as ingenious solutions to a housing shortage, but have now been condemned as appalling town planning and nothing but human-hating structures. There is little community spirit here and much loneliness.

Perhaps I am painting a gloomy picture and someone reading this who may be contemplating leaving home for England might be put off, but scenes of poverty, crime and neglect can be found in any city in the world.

Council estates and social housing, where people do not own their own homes, vary hugely around the country. Many are well-kept and life continues here on a relatively even keel most of the time. When Mrs Thatcher was Prime Minister (1979 to 1990), she encouraged people to buy their own council houses as a way of moving on from a life of dependency and to establish themselves on the property ladder. I think that it was a great idea. Having ownership of their home gives people a feeling of belonging and pride, and a desire to create and increase wealth for themselves.

When I first heard about council housing, I was in Manchester and the mother of one of the ladies who worked in the office had a council house. I just could not understand the whole concept of it, that even an ordinary working class person could rent a house at a subsidised rent. Later on, after my retirement, I was for a while a non-executive director on the Board of Newham Homes—a government controlled company. There I learnt a great deal about government's housing policies. The worst part of the whole policy was that that there was more unemployment among council housing tenants than elsewhere. Having a subsidised house and with other state benefits around, people appeared to become work shy. That is where my belief is clear—more social welfare makes people rely too much on state benefits.

The recent property boom in England has been phenomenal and it is still possible for people to make a fortune in the sector. The desire to buy your own home is not just the pleasure of owning your house but also knowing it is a sound investment. Most people believe that they are more likely to make money in property, even if they only own the one property they live in, than in the stock market. Having said that, the constantly rising prices make it difficult, if not impossible, for young people to get on the housing ladder. Owner-occupier rates in 13 London boroughs are below 50%. Of course, there have been ups and downs in the property market over the years and sometimes they can be very frightening, particularly if the market crashes when you have just taken a large mortgage on your house.

The drive to own your own property was particularly intoxicating during the boom times from the 1970s. People were encouraged to extend themselves and take out bigger and bigger mortgages. Problems occurred in the early and mid-1990s when recession hit the economy. There was rising unemployment and property prices fell. Home owners suddenly found themselves with mortgages higher than the value of the property. This was known as negative equity and led to many repossessions by the banks and building societies. A similar situation occurred again in 2007-08, when the sub-prime mortgage crisis in America hit the UK and other European countries, resulting in bank failures and the collapse of many other financial institutions.

But property always seems to bounce back, not in the least because not only in England but all over the world there is a housing shortage. This reminds me of a story, I heard in India some time ago, of a property tycoon who was on his death bed. He called his sons and advised them to always invest their surplus money in landed property whenever they found the right opportunity. On being asked the reason behind investing, especially in landed property, he replied, 'God has stopped making land a long time back but he is still producing people in large numbers, who need houses to live in.'

Although she was commenting on life in America in the 1960s, Malvina Reynolds' song, *Little Boxes*, performed by many artistes, is appropriate today:

> Little boxes on the hillside
> Little boxes made of ticky-tacky
> Little boxes on the hillside
> Little boxes all the same
> There's a green one and a pink one
> And a blue one and a yellow one
> And they're all made out of ticky-tacky
> And they all look just the same.

Prince Charles has been outspoken on many issues and housing and architecture is one of his favourite *bêtes noires*. He has built an entirely new village called Poundbury in Dorset, which is described on the Duchy of Cornwall's website as *'famous internationally as a pioneering example of urban development.'* He wanted to show that it was possible to build new towns with affordable houses for all pockets sympathetically and not as rows and rows of identical boxes.

In my experience in my early days in England and from what I hear now, bed-sit land is the realistic starting point for new visitors to England, students and sometimes for single persons moving from one job to another or until such time as they find some permanent accommodation. Again, prior to coming to England, I had not heard of this concept of bed-sit and did not know what it meant. Usually a family lets out one or two rooms in their house to supplement their income. Sometimes they are large houses converted into a number of independent rooms—known as multiple occupation properties. Students, being students, seem to be able to cope with crowded conditions, sharing all facilities and generally muddling along while they complete their studies. I suppose they endure this cramping lifestyle because they know it is only temporary. The very word 'temporary' snatches away the sense of belonging and eventually all traces of attachment from such dwellings. The word 'temporary' also provides solace to such persons, because they live in the knowledge that their present discomforts are not for ever and they will one day have better fortunes. Most of them do return home, which may be in England or further afield, and they begin the search for a job.

Having focused on the little boxes made of ticky-tacky, I would like to say that I respect them as they fulfil the basic need of many who cannot afford anything better. I have always learned to differentiate between needs and affordable needs. If human beings are given a free hand beyond affordability, many would settle for nothing less than Buckingham Palace for their home!

The reality is that most of us have to work up to lift ourselves gradually in our lives. A true home is where both the physical and psychological needs of a human being are fulfilled. To be able to zero in on such a home, one needs to make a balance between both needs, remembering well that every single human need can never be fulfilled, mainly because most of the time a person's needs are self-contradictory. I began my life in England some 60 years back, progressing from a shared room to a single room tenement and gradually up to a dream house of my choice in a community to which I belong. The beauty of England is that every sincere and capable person gets enough opportunity here to reach their coveted goal the way I achieved mine. So every person migrating to England and accepting it as their home has a sure chance of elevating themselves from a little box made of ticky-tacky to the home of their aspirations.

For the foreigner arriving in England for the first time, it can be difficult, as I experienced so many years ago. Invariably, people are attracted to quarters where they can meet their own kind, speak their own language and eat their own food, but in my experience that is a mistake. To get trapped, and that is how I view it, in such a narrowly focused community stifles any chance of absorbing English life and culture. Though a person may be able to communicate and express views with comparative ease within their own community, their growth and progress always remains bound within the parameters of one community only.

By contrast, if they mix and interact with other communities without bias, they enjoy better chances of widening their vision, knowledge and experience. In Mirza Ghalib's words, 'If a person is sad due to his own limited outlook, he should always look beyond his limitations. The multiple experiences offered by the external world would surely widen his narrow vision.'

Of course, it is usually a case of limited choices and you take what you can get, but when I arrived in Manchester I did not seek out fellow Indians—there weren't many in those days anyway—but I simply looked for lodgings wherever they were available. It did not occur to me to look first for another Indian and see if he or she would take me in.

I am convinced that visitors should mix and merge with their host country and its citizens as rapidly as possible and, to be frank, that is not happening in this country as much as I would like. Integration, to a large extent, is a myth and both hosts and visitors are the poorer for it. England has so much to offer—just go out and explore. But at the same time, I blame English politicians of different generations who have not encouraged integration over the years. In schools, children are encouraged and sometime taught their own language and allowed to wear their national dress and there are many other concessions. Grants are given to various community organisations to build their own mosques, temples and gurdwaras so as to maintain harmony. So far as I recall, similar policies were adopted in India by the ruling British—let everybody live within their own circle.

I would say this happens not only in England, but it is applicable to every country and its culture. Every community has its own customs and traditions, some of which may be considered good and some bad by others. However, the terms 'good' and 'bad' have no absolute justification as what one sees as 'good' may be looked down upon by another person. Therefore, instead of being critical of what we consider as 'bad', we always stand to benefit by accepting whatever we consider as 'good'. Vedic wisdom advises humans to inculcate *Madhukari Vritti* meaning 'the attitude of a honey bee'. 'Humans seeking enlightenment must focus on what they seek, forgetting all other hazards, just like honey bees do.' All a honey bee wants from a flower is honey and therefore it visits every flower, irrespective of its colour, fragrance and even thorns protecting it. If honey is good for the honey bee, it wastes no time in criticising the other undesired attributes of the flowers which it does not like.

If you really want to be part of English life, you will find that the beauty of the English countryside is not just the landscape, but also the rural architecture, the quaint old villages with timber frames and beams, old vicarages and occasionally, grand stately homes. Some do still stand *'to prove the upper classes still have the upper hand'* as Noel Coward sang. But more often than not, these places are either in the hands of a celebrity, or aristocratic families shorn of their estates to pay off death duties, or open to the public as living museums. These magnificent houses are full of history and should be regarded as such.

There is a relatively new type of development which I suppose has been largely adopted from the United States. These are the gated communities where access to whole estates is past a security guard. These properties are springing up throughout the country, usually just on the outskirts of affluent towns and cities. They are not quite country and not quite town. You do not have the mud and narrow lanes of a true rural life and you are sufficiently protected from the noise and possible crime of urban life. These are highly exclusive and expensive homes and somehow strangely devoid of real life. No one walks along the litter-free pavements apart from the occasional dog-walker with pooper-scooper in hand. Children are rarely seen playing on the precision mown front lawns because they are all safely in the house or in the extensive closed gardens at the back.

You have neighbours, but you never see them except by prior appointment or with a polite wave from the car as you pass each other on the road. Somewhere in between is the ideal, I suppose, a comfortable house but not in a mink-lined prison compound with guards on the gate. My childhood/adolescent experience in India, although times have changed, was that neighbourhood interaction there was in total contrast with the scenario in England, to the extent that at times it got close to interference. If you had your dinner out with family, your neighbour would definitely want to know every detail the next morning!

If you had exchanged a few harsh words with your spouse during night, your neighbour was sure to visit you the very next morning, on the lookout for gossip. Despite such inconveniences, if there was sickness in your household, your neighbour would gladly and voluntarily take care of your needs from morning tea to dinner, with folded hands. Mind you, the next day the entire neighbourhood would know how much service your neighbour had rendered to you while you were sick.

If this is the social scenario in the middle class neighbourhoods of India to which I once belonged, the affluent class is more given to aloofness and takes pride in telling you that they do not know who their next door neighbour is.

Privacy and knowing your rights is just as common in England as anywhere else in the world, but sometimes it goes to extremes.

Wherever the English choose to live, they preserve their little patch with pride. 'An Englishman's home is his castle,' they say and despite so many little bureaucratic intrusions into their private life, they will fiercely resist any attempt to undermine their defences. The principle of those rights dates back to the earliest English Common Law. The early English jurist, Sir Edward Coke (1552–1634) is quoted as saying, '*A man's house is his castle - et domus sua cuique tutissimum refugium*' (*One's home is the safest refuge for all*). I believe it was an argument for self-defence if an intruder broke in.

Lastly, and because this is a story about my England, we should explore some of the idiosyncratic lifestyles that you can encounter here. Although not unique to England, a life on the ocean, or at least floating quietly in a barge moored on a canal, is regarded by some of the English as heaven. I have had quite a few English friends—mostly professional—who owned boats and enjoyed being on them for days on end. Houseboats provide an idyllic life if you like that sort of thing. You can either remain moored in one spot or travel around the country, along the network of canals, many of which take you right through the heart of major cities. This is akin to the boat houses, a great tourist attraction at the Dal Lake in Srinagar, Kashmir, where the boats are converted into compact residential units and fully furnished. Similar boat houses are also seen in Kerala back waters.

All along the river Thames in London, old warehouses have been converted into penthouse pads and luxurious flats and offices. Rivers have always attracted development, for obvious commercial reasons, and happily for London anyway, great efforts have been made to clean up the rivers, which in turn have attracted the developers again. There, I admire the English for being so innovative and enterprising.

The lure of the sea is a powerful one and seaside towns like Brighton are growing continuously, with smart luxury apartment conversions commanding high prices. Before lighthouses became largely automated, some people lived and worked in them and now disused lighthouses are snapped up whenever they come on the market.

An Englishman's Home Is His Castle

But the reality for most people is a progression from rented flat, shared house, your first own home with a sizeable mortgage and a series of buying and selling deals until, finally, you are satisfied. Once you have your home, regardless of size, you really a feel part of the neighbourhood, somehow you feel you have certain rights and you feel you belong. I believe this is a dream worth chasing. Your home does not have to have turrets and battlements, but it must provide you with a sense of pride—after all it is your castle.

I visit India twice a year, mostly to meet my brothers, sisters and other relatives. I do enjoy their company but I never feel at home there. Over the past 60 years, I have become so much 'An Englander' that I feel out of place even in my so-called homeland.

It was this feeling I experienced while I was visiting India that prompted me to write this book on England—my true home that I hold so dear to my heart!

Receiving 'Freedom' of City of London

7

The Mysteries of the English Education System

> Education has produced a vast population able to read but unable to distinguish what is worth reading.
>
> G. M. Trevelyan

Think of the pinnacle of education anywhere in the world and most people would think of the two great English universities of Oxford and Cambridge; so famous that they are often conjoined as Oxbridge. The battle to win a place at these universities is probably the most stressful test a young person is likely to face in their entire life. It takes months of additional preparation at school, separate entry examinations on top of the basic, perfect entry requirements and a period of prolonged misery in the family home, waiting to hear whether or not a place has been achieved. The reward is priceless—an Oxbridge degree is usually an automatic *entrée* into any job.

Even as a young student in India, I knew about these great seats of learning and I assumed that England had mastered all elements of education. But even as we move through the 21st century, it seems the English are still agonising over the best way to educate their young.

Since my arrival in the late 1950s, I have witnessed and experienced the different ideas of education in this country. On the face of it, everything is perfectly straightforward; there is private and state education. Among the well-to-do Indians here, it is common to talk about which school your daughter or son goes to. If they do not go to a private school, you may have no status in that society. At the end of their schooldays, they might go astray. However, it still means a lot today to Indian and other people of our class that our children go to a private school.

This is perhaps not surprising as so much of the formal way of life finds its roots in the days of the English Raj. My parents were not in a position to send any of their children to a private school. We all went to ordinary state assisted schools, which were partly funded by the government, where we had to pay some fees. I remember in my early days of schooling, sitting on the floor of a classroom. I also have memories of corporal punishment and twice being thrown out of school as my father could not pay the fees.

I was, therefore, surprised to learn that it is compulsory for all English children aged between 5 and 16 to attend school, and that corporal punishment was practically non-existent. As a matter of fact, I learnt later on that a teacher could be disciplined or even prosecuted for inflicting physical punishment on a school child. I do not know how it is now in schools in India, but I remember being beaten by teachers—sometimes unnecessarily. I was very happy when I got to university, where there was no corporal punishment. We were then treated as grown-ups, or should I say, human beings.

English schools in the state sector are financed by the government and either managed by the local authorities or the so-called Grant Maintained Schools and recently Academies, can run their own affairs. There are no school fees. After primary level, secondary education for 11 years onwards is in comprehensive schools, although some grammar schools which select the more able children, do still exist.

In short, England has a state system which is mainly comprehensive, but there are places which still retain the old selection system of secondary modern and grammar schools. Initially, when I arrived in England, I was not concerned about the English education system. I did not take much interest in it. However, I got married to a school teacher and our daughter went to a private school. In later years, I was to become more involved in the world of education, taking on roles in governance and in encouraging young people to take advantage of the career and life opportunities available in their local community and beyond.

Grammar schools are a peculiar English anomaly; a splendid English compromise even. Grammar schools have a terrific reputation, but were and still are accused of taking the cream of students out of the normal state sector. They came about as a result of the old division—the workers and those who thought they could do better. After World War II, schooling was re-organised into secondary moderns, which were essentially for children who wanted a trade, and grammar, for those who wanted to pursue higher education, university and ultimately the professions. During the Labour government era of the 1960s, a decision was taken that every child would enjoy complete education, and the comprehensives were born. However, local authorities were allowed to make the change at their own speed, so, consequently, today some areas still have comprehensives running alongside grammar schools.

Formal education, after infant level, in private schools begins as early as seven years of age at preparatory school, before children take their Common Entrance Examination and move on to Public School from 13 to 18 years. That is the pattern our daughter followed. I left the education of my daughter in my wife's hands as she had extensive experience of the system, having been a school teacher in a state school. Personally, I wanted my daughter to go to an ordinary state school and become part of our local community and broader society. There are advantages and disadvantages of private education. Parents who decide to opt for private education face ever increasing fees, but private schools are self-governing and usually have better facilities than state schools.

Entry into private schools is very tough and the names of children are usually put down at birth for the parents' school of choice. This is no guarantee of entry, but if you are late putting your child's name down for a particular school, in all probability you will be disappointed, regardless of your child's educational level or your financial ability to pay the fees.

In the past, children of nobility would be educated at home by a governess, but gradually great public schools like Eton and Harrow were established. A few were established in the 15th and 16th centuries, but most of them started by the 18th and 19th centuries, by when it was commonplace for all boys from privileged backgrounds to be despatched to boarding schools, where they would learn to mix with others of a similar background. Conditions in those early days were spartan. *Tom Brown's School Days* by Thomas Hughes recounts all there is to know and more about life in those days. All terribly English, tough and designed to stiffen that upper lip.

It is interesting to note that, originally, Eton College was founded by King Henry VI to provide free education for 70 poor scholars. There is nothing impoverished about most of the parents who send their children there today. That is not a criticism, it is a fact of life. There are many parents, particularly Indians, who one would call middle class or even lower class, who would spend their last penny to ensure their offspring get the best education money can buy. And a similar type of private education system was developed in India by the British during the days of the Raj. The senior civil servants and army officers sent their children to boarding schools—my uncle, who was a colonel in the army, had sent all his children to such establishments. And to this day, this system of private education and boarding schools is still flourishing in India.

It would be fair to say that life in the private education sector has, by and large, continued smoothly, but it is the comparative chaos in the state sector which is still troubling governments of all political persuasions. Parents are faced with seemingly endless change and insurmountable hurdles—11 plus tests, Key Stage tests, the lottery of a school's catchment area and the chances of living near a good school and even getting a child to school safely every day, particularly if both parents are working. When I sit on an admissions panel, I see that so often parents are disappointed with their application for their children, as they do not fall within certain categories recommended by the government.

English schools have begun looking abroad for solutions, which seems an incredible state of affairs for a nation steeped in learning. The French International Baccalaureate is now in use in a number of schools here, for the simple reason that some teachers felt the traditional narrow selection of A levels was just that—too narrow, restricting a child's outlook too soon in life. Many students are taking multiple A levels these days and it is not unusual for their subjects to be highly focused, particularly in the sciences. In the Baccalaureate system, all students study the same broad set of subjects, which in my view gives them a commendably broader basis, either for their further studies at university or for their chosen career.

So far as I can remember, education has always been a political hot potato. There is no doubt that standards in English schools are falling—the so-called dumbing down effect—to such an extent that universities are having to modify their courses, just to bring budding businessmen, mathematicians, scientists or academics to a basic level of expertise. Even the ability to express themselves coherently in written English is apparently almost beyond many students.

There is also a new phenomenon occurring in England as a result of her open door policy and multi-culturalism, and it is causing serious problems. There are schools in some cities, where English is a second language and where English may not even be spoken in class. If one combines this with a home life for children where again English may not be spoken, and where some members of the family do not go out to work, then you have the makings of a divided society, not a truly cosmopolitan nation rejoicing in the diversity such a mix of cultures has to offer.

In these situations, you cannot even rely on television to bring some English into the home, because the wonder of satellite television means there is probably a different channel for every ethnic community in the land.

These are issues which are recognised by all political parties and the challenge for them is to find a solution without delay, before new generations of school children find themselves ill-prepared for their lives ahead. The sad part of it all is that it was England who gave the English language, the language of modern education, to the world. I wonder if England will look at the Indian education system, which is producing high quality graduates, year after year. On the other hand, during my recent visits to India, I noticed that among the growing prosperous middle class, that English had nearly become the first language. In these homes, parents speak English with their children, who go to private schools where English is taught as a first language. Let us not forget that among the hundreds of millions of people in India, there are nearly 300 million middle class Indians and it is estimated that by the year 2020, India will be the largest English speaking country in the world.

I would like to look at the whole question of the boarding school—the English are either for it or against it and often it has no bearing on the sort of experience they themselves had.

It is not unknown for a child (usually sons, not daughters) to be despatched to boarding school as young as seven, but usually eight. That child will remain at school, parted from the parents and siblings apart from holidays and occasional days out during the term, for the next ten years. Even then they may go to university for another three years before launching themselves on the unsuspecting world, having spent more time away from home than in it!

I have an English friend who was recounting this experience to a French lady as she was driving and she nearly crashed the car, so shocked was she by the seeming inhumanity and cruelty. And yet it seems to work. In Sweden, they don't even start any sort of formal education until a child is ten or so, let alone send their offsprings somewhere far away, only to return as young adults.

Much has been written about the pros and cons of such a system, the psychological impact of being torn from the family home and thrust among complete strangers, who may or may not like you, but for many English it is a fact of life. It makes you or it breaks you and I suspect the English would not have it any other way. A similar sort of situation exists in India among the upper middle class who despatch their children to boarding schools which are growing in number every year because there is so much demand for them. The general experience is that children coming out of such schools do well in life. My brother in India sent his two children to boarding school - his son to Dehradun and his daughter to Shimla - and they both have done well in life so much so that the son later came to the world famous London School of Economics in London and the prestigious University of Harvard in the USA.

During my early days in India, a degree was a must for every middle class child, even though he/she went to an ordinary school. They have always been accessible without having to pay a fee. Apart from ordinary universities where you will get degrees in all type of subjects, there were specialised universities for medicine, engineering, tourism and hotel management, IT and so on. Getting into a special university was difficult, as you needed to hold a high class degree from an ordinary university before you could apply for entrance into these speciality institutions. My current understanding is that these specialist universities have become very overpowering and domineering. However, on the plus side, these specialist universities have produced an army of specialist graduates who have become the envy of the world.

About the universities again here in England, another debate rages. The Labour Government, before it lost power in 2010, set a target of 50% of all school leavers going to university. But many question the wisdom of such an ambition; what is the purpose of just going to university? As Lee Rudolph, the American Professor of Mathematics, said, 'No one wants a good education. Everyone wants a good degree.' Many students will admit that they do, in fact, go to university just for the degree, without any real idea of what they plan to do with it when they graduate, or what they plan to do with their life, generally.

The central organisation for processing university applications in England, UCAS, has an ever growing book of possible degree courses available for study at English universities. This is testimony to the insatiable demand for some sort of degree, but perhaps one has to question the value of some of those degree courses. Universities have to survive and fee paying foreign students alone do not help to balance the books. The lack of interest in many of the science courses as compared with some of the softer, easier options has resulted in distinguished departments closing through lack of support. This must surely be a concern, as talented professors find themselves struggling to pursue their specialisation or, worse still, leaving the country for more lucrative pastures.

In many countries, the science courses are over-subscribed. It is to the Far East that people are looking for breakthroughs in medical discovery. Should we be resting on our laurels in England, or re-considering our priorities? This country has a unique history of learning and it should be cherished and nurtured before irreparable damage is done.

England my love, wake up darling to the realities of the present day world!

8

The English at Work

> There are two kinds of people,
> those who do the work and those who take the credit.
> Try to be in the first group; there is less competition there.
>
> Indira Gandhi

The Greeks considered work to be a curse. Their word for work was *ponos*, which is connected to the Latin *poena*, meaning sorrow. P. D. Antony, in his book *The Ideology of Work*, said Plato and Aristotle were clear that labourers worked to leave the elite free to consider higher subjects like art, philosophy and politics.

But for us mere mortals, this remains the age-old conundrum—do we live to work or do we work to live? I think the contrast between the two is most vividly displayed here in England.

No-one would dispute the work ethic of the Indians. When the East India Company was ruling India, and a ruler it was, there were countless records praising the hard work, quick learning and industry of the indigenous work force. Moving quickly to the present day, there are just as many stories of how Indians have come to England, with little to their names, and have built substantial businesses, turning themselves into millionaires in the process.

There could not be any greater contrast than with the English approach to life, which is an approach that many immigrants are also adopting. On the whole, excluding the exceptional 'get up and go' entrepreneurs (and there are a fair number of those), the English take on a more relaxed approach to life. They are more in the US President Ronald Reagan's camp. He said, 'It is true hard work never killed anyone, but I figure, why take the chance?' A Hindu philosopher would rather say that it is my hard work that would achieve Nirvana for me.

For some English people the thought of discussing business at a social occasion would be considered vulgar, although this is less and less the case. An Indian on the other hand will jump straight in and ask you how you make your money and grill you on turn-over, business opportunities and will certainly be seeking potential links and joint ventures. In other cultures, this may not be the case. It can be a bit overwhelming for the uninitiated.

Having said that, we know that the English invented the term 'the Protestant work ethic' back in the 17th century. The idea was that by working hard, we did well and generated wealth, which was God's way of blessing our diligence. The corollary, of course, was that the indolent and lazy were poor and undeserving of the good things in life. So it became acceptable to have vast wealth—US industrialist J. D. Rockefeller said, 'God gave me money.' For some, of course, it has gone much beyond and money is their god.

The compulsion to work ever harder has become a sickness of modern times. In Japan, as well as in some other countries, where loyalty to their companies is legendary, workers put in long hours of unpaid overtime. Many workers seem to say with their warm smiles that they enjoyed it all and long hours did not bother them—possibly because 90% of them had no other pastime. Work was their life.

I was reading some advice to young teachers contemplating working in the Far East. The article was trying to explain the differences in culture and work ethic. The author encapsulated the difference as being Westerners will work for themselves, while the East Asians will be more group motivated—'we' rather than

'I'. However, I am not sure of that as I feel that the modern generation, middle class people still veer more towards 'I'.

But back to the English work attitudes and environment. I think it is still the case that whereas the English will work hard, once off duty they will relax, go out partying and probably unwind over a few drinks. In the city of London, this would be quite a few drinks. Indians will probably return home, maybe even to their parents' home, and continue discussing business. In all probability it will be the family business so there is no break. Again, I feel old family feelings are dying out and Western habits and culture are creeping in and gradually taking over Asian, too.

The question is why are they working? If work is the driver, what is the motivation? The Asian is working to make the business even more successful, there is no finishing line and there is a loyalty to the family business. The Indian may well have been entrusted with a particular division of the company and they in turn will be looking to pass on an element of the operation to their children.

In my experience, there does not usually seem to be any of that loyalty with the Western workers, unless of course they are in a family business, but that would be the exception rather than the rule.

So, it is my belief that, generally speaking, an English worker's loyalty is to himself or herself. I have to say, though, that in my formal experience when I was running my own practice, I had a staff of some 14 people, of which half were English. I found that English women workers were much devoted to me and were concerned about my progress. I built up my practice for many years and a lot of credit goes to my staff. I would particularly single out the English women on my staff, who not only worked hard, but also made sure that our clients were looked after so that they remained our clients.

Admittedly, among the older generation of English workers, a certain loyalty exists. But I notice lack of loyalty even in the gardener who tends our house garden. His loyalty is to himself and this type of loyalty is seen at all levels. Just consider what happens at the end of every financial year when the top City earners receive their huge bonuses. Once the cheque has cleared into their accounts, the next booming business is of the Head Hunters. The highest achievers put their names in the ring and will be quite happy to move to another, even a rival firm if the deal is right. They are driven by money. The high-flyers in the City do, of course, work ferocious hours and would be expected to work weekends and cancel holidays at short notice to complete a deal, but essentially they are no different from the factory worker—they are working for their pay-cheque, not for the good of the business.

So if the goal is wealth, is there room for anything else a little more elevating? Many of the really high flyers in the Asian Rich list still find time to make regular, if not daily, visits to their temples. Some may even have endowed those temples.

Now I cannot claim to be a religious man, nor to be able to look into the minds of such people, but it seems to suggest that they believe there is more to life than work. At least there are other priorities or possibly these visits to temples are more of a family tradition or to fulfil a request or honour the memory of their parents. For example, when I am in India, I try to visit my sister, who never married and lives in Vrindavan, a holy place. The visit is more a family ritual rather than a feeling of real devotion to Lord Krishna whose birthplace it is.

Basically, wealth creates its own culture. Although it may become your god, having wealth can also enable you to devote time to God. As I said earlier and in my previous book, Hindu culture or religion does not decry the creation of wealth for yourself. Neither does English culture. It is godly to be rich and to be able to help others.

I talk of religion and philosophy in other chapters. In relation to work, it is surprising how many religious images depicting holy people from the past you will find in Asian offices. Again, this is an outward sign that they believe there is some greater force at work or to concur with family tradition. In my experience working up and down the country, you will not find a single religious symbol in any Westerner's office. However, concessions are made to Muslim workers in factories, where special prayer areas are set aside, but it has absolutely no bearing on the running of the factory.

If the Greeks considered work a curse, the modern day curse is probably that your work identifies you. The first question you are asked after your name and where you live or hail from is, what do you do? That is because this places you suitably in the social order. You may deliver milk because you like the outdoor life and the freedom the inevitable early shifts give you to do other things during the day, but if the person standing next to you says they are a merchant banker, your relative place in the social order gets decided. You are what you do. Often, you are what you are born to be and that is your luck because that is the life to which you were born. But, in England, there is nothing to stop the same person becoming a successful merchant banker or business owner, so long as they are willing to take steps to change their outlook and to work hard.

Sharon Beder, author of *Selling the Work Ethic*, puts it succinctly, 'We need to find new ways of judging and valuing each other that are not work and income dependent. It would be a sad world indeed if producing goods for consumption was the highest goal to which humans could aspire.'

In truth, what it comes down to is if you are at the bottom of the heap you will probably work harder to improve yourself, whereas if life is relatively cushy why bother too much? No one is immune to a foreign worker taking their position. In India, workers from different states of India who speak completely different languages, come from completely different traditions and practise completely different forms of religion, often move to more prosperous states in search of work. Most of them leave families behind in their birth states. Immigration to other lands has been deep-rooted in human nature. There used to be complaints about the Irish who came to dig the roads, there were complaints about Asians taking over all the corner shops and who were prepared to stay open all day, every day and now there are concerns about Eastern Europeans.

It really is the same the world over. I read some time ago about a mine in Kentucky where they were prepared to relax their strict rules about being fluent in English because *'the work ethic of the Eastern Kentucky worker has declined from where it once was.'*

I do not know the precise circumstances of this mine, but it often happens that the employers become fed up meeting the demands or the rights of their workforce. Everyone today knows their rights, even little schoolchildren, but no one seems to be aware of their responsibilities.

It comes back to the question, why are we working? What are the pressures? The pressures are clear enough—peer pressures. We must have the latest car, the latest electronic gizmo, sport the latest fashion. The pressures are relentless and are driven by a consumerist society. The more we consume, the harder someone has to work to keep producing what we think we need. But we are simply being made to think that way by the advertising on our brand new television which is probably telling us our TV is already out of date!

It helps, of course, if you are doing the work you like. Dale Carnegie, the arch motivator, the best-selling author of *How to Win Friends and Influence People*, said, 'Are you bored with life? Then throw yourself into some work you believe in with all your heart, live for it, die for it, and you will find happiness that you had thought could never be yours.' And it is true to the end. Hindu and Buddhist scriptures are full of sayings like this. Doing your Karma you enjoy with full devotion will bring true happiness to you.

At the same time, the absence of work can be terribly debilitating. I think of the miners in the Welsh valleys whose entire existence was devoted to the local mine, who were suddenly without work; or workers from the now virtually defunct English car manufacturing or steel works. At first there was anger, then frustration, then, for those who could not re-train, terrible boredom. It saps a person's strength and pride. It seems that a human being needs to work. From my personal experience in my homeland, I can vouch that I could not get a job after graduation. Sending applications and getting rejection replies just made me sick. Had this continued, I may have developed an inferiority complex which would have created a negative personality within me. And how elated I felt when I got a job in Manchester as an articled clerk!

Having a job that I enjoyed created a new energy and new purpose to my life.

Work is an important part of human life; if you enjoy what you are doing, it is good fortune. In this respect, I would like to say that women are lucky. Having a child and bringing it up is itself an essential and hard work and that can provide great satisfaction and a certain purpose to a woman's life. And of course, especially in recent years in England, women have been successful in balancing their family lives with careers—so they are benefiting twice from their family and professional roles.

Will the treadmill run on forever or will someone one day say, 'Stop!' It will require a terrible grinding of gears. If it is in our nature to work hard, as I believe it is, how do we stop? Should we stop? Maybe the answer is to continue working hard, but to do something else with the money we earn, to alter our motivation. We can only eat three meals a day; we can only drive one car at a time and even that car we cannot drive very fast because of all the other cars on the road. Maybe the Greeks had it right in part—they kept their minds clear to focus on higher things! Perhaps the reward will come in later life. We are all living longer and, generally speaking, we are fitter in our old age. The power of the grey pound is hugely attractive to the advertisers who are targeting the pensioners to tap into their nest eggs.

There is something rather sad, even tragic, that we work hard simply to earn the right to have fun in our twilight years. Surely, the whole of life is for living, not just one small part of it.

My philosophy is to make the most of my days, such as they are. I worked hard and now I intend to reap the rewards, treating myself to the little indulgences I believe I have earned. Until someone can come up with a better way of conducting one's life, the 'work now play later' option is the only one on offer and there is plenty of opportunity for it in my England my love.

9

The English Love of Sport

There's a breathless hush in the Close tonight –
Ten to make and the match to win –
A bumping pitch and a blinding light,
An hour to play and the last man in.
And it's not for the sake of the ribboned coat,
Or the selfish hope of a season's fame,
But his Captain's hand on his shoulder smote –
'Play up! Play up! And play the game!'

Vitaï Lampada, Sir Henry John Newbolt

Cricket is such an English concept, so much so that when someone behaves in an unsporting way, it is defined as 'just not cricket'—the ultimate gentleman's and lady's game. Cricket itself, as we will see later, has moved further away from the ideals of polite conduct, but nevertheless, the standards remain for those who want to uphold them and those standards were first set in England.

Sport is so embedded in English culture that phrases relating to sport are widespread in the English language and are in everyday use. 'Just not cricket' is one such phrase, and a closer inspection of the language uncovers numerous other examples like batting on a sticky wicket, playing with a straight bat, saved by the bell, he's completely snookered, a level playing field. The list is almost endless, and it says a great deal about the values of English society.

I was never a sportsperson of any description, but I can appreciate achievement when I see it. I applauded the extraordinary feat of the then rookie English Formula One Driver, Lewis Hamilton, who at the age of 22 achieved third place on the podium in his debut race in Melbourne in 2007. I applauded even more his obvious modesty and noted how in every interview he praised the enormous back-up team behind him. He has since gone on to win the Formula One World Championship three times and is now a major player in the sport.

Sport today is masterminded by agents, managers, sponsors and a veritable army of hangers-on. It is serious money and there is no room for amateurs or amateur notions of simply enjoying taking part, without the desire to win. But the exceptions, like young Lewis Hamilton, prove that you can have both; he clearly has a steely determination and focus and yet he has managed to keep his feet firmly on the ground and retained a delightful modesty which you find in people who have a gift but scarcely realise it.

However, sport in England shows another, less appealing side. Cheating in sport—particularly Association Football—is now so common that it is called a professional foul, a shameful oxymoron which means the players judge that it is in the best interests of their own team to scythe down another player who is threatening to score. Even though the referee will award a penalty against the offending players, they would rather suffer that indignity than be a goal down.

But let us not be rude about football—perhaps the national sport in England—because the same applies to most major sports throughout the world. Even cricket is not without its boorish behaviour; every batsman and woman expects to suffer 'sledging' when they arrive at the crease—non-stop verbal abuse to put them off their stroke.

Just as England gave the world the English language, this country gave the world so many sports, but in their delightfully amateurish fashion the English have seen themselves being overcome in so many of them by countless nations. The same goes for English language usage, which has better standards in other nations. I must not be unfair to the many gold, silver and bronze medallists that England has produced and, after all, it is a relatively small country, but I am not sure that is the whole answer.

I have a sneaking suspicion that, as a nation, the English do not have the killer instinct when it comes to sport—at least not in sufficient quantity consistently to top any medals chart. Is there something in their character which holds them back, a sort of in-built control mechanism? The English still enjoy taking part in sport. On the whole, not many of them are fighting to improve their way of life, like some street-fighter who sees boxing as the only way out of the gutter. There are some tough gutters in the UK, but not as many as in the USA or China. Consequently, you do not get that build-up of pressure to create competition. Is life too comfortable for the majority?

Tim Henman, the archetypal 'Gentleman Jim' tennis player, came from a refined upper-middle class background. He was polite to umpires, polite to his opponents. He did not snarl and you felt he was faintly embarrassed when he tried to punch the air to show some emotion. His parents, who watched all his matches, applauded politely without whoops and shouts. Poor old Tim was never going to win Wimbledon, there was no fire in his belly and no anger, all of which meant Henman was always going to be just a very good tennis player, a delight to be with, popular with the crowds on Wimbledon's Henman Hill, but never the Champion. Since his retirement, he has become an accomplished broadcaster and commentator and is a respected and trusted expert in his sport. So his ability to get on with everyone in and beyond his sport has certainly paid dividends to him.

Now the home crowd does have a new hero in Andy Murray and you can see the contrasts in style and attitude. Murray, of course, is a Scot and there is a very big difference between the Scots and the English. Murray prowls about in his cap, getting angry with himself, mostly, but sometimes with his racket and the occasional doubtful umpire's decision. He seems to have something to prove. In his television interviews, you do not get the Henman warmth and smile. Murray appears to be on a mission and that focus and determination has seen him beat all-time greats like Roger Federer. Murray has proved that combining skills with athletic ability and aggression is a winning formula, and his tally of titles to date includes Wimbledon twice, the US Open and the Olympics, as well as being the pivotal player in Great Britain's victory in the Davis Cup in 2015.

Even with rose tinted glasses about England and its way of life, sport can throw up some pretty nasty acts and now I am thinking particularly of the fans. Immediately I can hear howls of protest—the trouble makers are not the real fans. Maybe not, but they are part of the caravan which follows sports teams around the world. The worst, of course, are football hooligans—to give them their proper name—who have no real interest in the games and just use them as an occasion for violence. Sadly, England has an unenviable reputation here. All one can say is that the worst of the violence seems to be a thing of the past, with only an occasional flare-up.

It is fair to say that the trouble is not just among the fans. There are many instances of foul play on the pitch. The French player Zinedine Zidane's notorious head butt on the Italian defender Marco Materazzi in the 2006 World Cup final must rate as the most watched offence on a football field, but there are countless examples where sportsmen and women have let themselves and their sport down. But all these negatives are greatly outweighed by the positives from sport and sport in England, despite everything, is surely a fine ambassador.

The English are sports mad and with the growing emphasis in the 21st century on leisure activities, this is probably just as well. Increasingly, sport is seen as a career option not just for Physical Education (PE) instructors at school, but for advanced study in universities in subjects such as sports psychology and sports therapy. The courses are endless. Just type in the word 'sports' on Google UK and you get in excess of 125 million search results.

There was, what I might call a blip, among state schools during the 1970s when playing fields were being sold off as head teachers tried to supplement their schools' income. There also seemed to be a lack of interest in the whole business of keeping fit; teachers were reluctant to stay on after school to coach teams as they were already under severe time pressure, or perhaps they just could not find youngsters interested. That all seems to have changed and the importance of fitness has been recognised. Many schools are chasing Lottery funding to reinstate facilities, which not only benefit schools but also local communities. The Olympic success of athletes like Dame Kelly Holmes has shown that anyone, regardless of background, can achieve great heights. Dame Kelly is now a sort of roving ambassador for sport, travelling the country and encouraging youngsters.

People are also getting fitter, by which I mean when they reach retirement age, they still feel fit and active. The so-called grey pound is very valuable, with pensioners more likely to take up a new hobby or sport in their later years than perhaps our parents would have done. And I am not just talking about a little gentle walking or sightseeing. These pensioners are taking up activities like skiing, snow-boarding and so on.

Sport is a great leveller and it is available to all. The class distinctions which were so clearly made in sports have been largely eradicated—today, if you are good, you are in the team. There was a time when Rugby Union was for gentlemen and Association Football was for the rest, to put it politely. Looking from the outside, I notice certain shifts. While what everyone understands as the 'middle classes' are unlikely to play professional football, rugby is open to all. But rugby itself has its own divide between League and Union. Now that both are professional, it is not uncommon to see players switching between the two. Nevertheless, Rugby League remains a predominantly Northerners' game, while Union is firmly rooted in the south of England. Class distinctions still exist today—even in sport, it seems.

The point I would like to make though, is the days of strolling up to Twickenham, pipe in hand, having a quick chat with your chums and then running on to score a try are just wonderful oddities from the past. Professionalism, strict training regimes and focus have turned these sports into full time careers in England.

Where all this leaves the amateurs of the Olympics, I do not know. I heard the games described as a 'cheat-fest for drug takers' on television recently, which was obviously over the top, but the line between amateur and professional athletes has probably long been bridged. Tennis, after all, is an Olympic sport but all players are professionals. The athletes just have to fudge the issue of whether or not they are officially sponsored or just on an extended sabbatical from their normal employment.

This is what sport can do for you—it can lift spirits as a stirring anthem resounds around the stadium and it can pull a country together as a national team battles against impossible odds to win the game in the dying moments.

England should take pride in what it has given the world in sport.

With Queen's Representative

10

The English Holiday Culture

A perpetual holiday is a good working definition of hell.

George Bernard Shaw

The 19th century businessman and entrepreneur Thomas Cook was probably responsible for the English holiday phenomenon of the packaged tour, although, of course, it was all much more refined in those days.

To be accurate, some would say the medieval pilgrimage was the real beginning of taking a break from work. Pilgrims were in search of some religious experience and the word 'holiday' derives from 'holy day'. In the Roman Catholic church, they have Holy Days of Obligation when the faithful are supposed to attend mass—these were originally the only days of rest for the labourers toiling in the fields.

In the 16th century and right up to the middle of the 19th century, wealthy English people went on what was known as the 'Grand Tour' of European cities; parents, often accompanied by their growing children, would soak up the culture, educating their children in the process and introducing them to another world. Most upper class girls at that time would have had a very closeted life, with governesses at home and would not even have been to school.

This tour was like a finishing school—establishments which used to be popular for young ladies looking for that European polish, before the advent of the more free-for-all form of travel we are accustomed to today. In today's world, we have the phenomenon of the gap year in between school and university, which is common to many countries.

In 1841, Thomas Cook arranged for a group of people to travel from Leicester to Loughborough by train, just 11 miles away and the packaged holiday was born. By an Act of Parliament in 1871, every worker was given the right to an annual holiday, although at that stage holidays abroad were strictly for the upper classes.

No review of the English on holiday would be complete without a nod towards the holiday camps, with such famous names as Butlin's and Pontin's. The golden age for such organised, even structured breaks was in the 1950s and 1960s, although the very idea of going on holiday at all was novel enough after the deprivations of the Second World War. In fact, Billy Butlin opened his first camp in Skegness as early as 1936, followed by another two years later in Clacton. The camps were requisitioned by the military during the Second World War, but Billy Butlin saw the opportunity. He built other camps with holidays in mind and allowed them to be used by the military, with the agreement that he would be allowed to buy them back after the war. By the end of hostilities, Butlin had five holiday camps ready for the holiday-makers. These camps were unique in many ways. They could accommodate huge numbers in one location—between 2,000 and 5,000 people, there was organised entertainment and there was a permanent team of official hosts on hand to keep the party atmosphere going. These hosts were the famous Redcoats.

What Butlin was doing was following up the very English delight in camping. But Butlin also recognised that, when the inevitable rain started falling, holiday makers looked miserable and at a loss as to what to do. So not only was food plentiful and affordable, but there was also something to do under cover and protection from the elements.

Fred Pontin, who had gained experience running camps and providing catering for the military during the Second World War, was another pioneer in this field. His camps were smaller than Butlin's and advertised as 'Holiday Camps for the Connoisseur'.

The modern version of these camps, where everything is laid out in a controlled environment, is probably the Center Parcs concept, which actually began in Holland some 30 years ago. The idea was to offer a holiday destination on a year round basis, located in woodland. But this is not really roughing it. High quality accommodation is available in fully equipped villas, apartments and lodges and there are shops, sport and leisure activities, as well as restaurants and bars. It does not matter what the weather is outside, there is always somewhere to go and something to do inside. It is possible to spend your whole holiday without putting your nose outside the door!

English seaside towns have always been the preferred destinations for most holiday makers, and these began to prosper as the rail network improved, bringing them approachable from the bigger cities. As early as the 18th century, spa towns sprang up as people went in search of cures for all sorts of ailments from the natural spring waters to be found in places like Bath. Today, seaside towns are still enormously popular and the beaches in the summer months are crowded, helped in part by the hotter summers England is now enjoying.

I should also mention the caravan, which is either hated by countless motorists caught in long lines of slow-moving holiday traffic, or adored for providing at least some of the comforts and privacy of your own home. Caravans are much more elaborate than the little boxes on wheels of the past, with only very basic facilities. They can sleep five or more and the National Caravan Council estimates that caravanning in all its forms is worth £1 billion to the UK economy.

But while the 'masses' were travelling to the likes of Brighton, Blackpool and Southend, at the other end of the economic spectrum, the well-to-do made trips to the French Riviera where in time the *beau monde* from the film industry would gather to see and be seen.

Many people may have forgotten, but to be a BOAC (British Overseas Airways Corporation, the fore-runner to British Airways) air hostess was a highly desirable job even in the better families. Always elegant and striking in their high-heeled shoes, air hostesses were the very epitome of glamour, particularly when inter-continental air travel started. Now being a member of the cabin crew is little more than being a glorified attendant, delivering mass-produced meals—if you can get a meal—to unappreciative, often over-demanding passengers, who would probably behave quite differently at home!

So how and when did the rot set in or, if you take the alternate point of view, when were the skies opened up to all? Sir Freddie Laker, the British entrepreneur, was the first to introduce the concept of a 'no-frills' service, with tickets available on the day and a restricted in-flight service. Others like EasyJet, Ryanair and Virgin Atlantic were to follow his lead with spectacular, if at times controversial, success. But it was Sir Freddie's 'Skytrain' which proved it was possible to offer a cut-price transatlantic service, and budget travel for all was born.

The English love the extraordinary deals, which have become the norm. Such deals encourage business people in London, who once may have relied on a phone call or a letter, to jump on a plane, fly up to Scotland for a couple of hours' meeting and then be back at home to watch the evening news. Holiday makers can now fly to America for less than the price of the rail fare between major cities in England.

But passengers are not always so happy when things go wrong with budget airlines. There usually is no back-up plane when a fault develops, there is no flexibility for passengers arriving late to check in, there are tight restrictions on luggage and there is no free food or drink.

Some of the cut-price airlines do not quite deliver you to the city centres they claim to serve and you have to get on a train or bus to reach the heart of the town. This somewhat loose definition of Rome, Milan, Paris and other destinations has now been tightened up and the airlines have to be specific about the fact that you are really arriving in a remote suburb.

However, one must not knock this down, because many of these distant airfields have expanded rapidly, created thousands of jobs and breathed new life into dying dormitory towns. 'London Stansted', in reality a short train ride from the centre of London, is now England's fastest growing airport. A new terminal was opened in 1991, but that is now creaking under the pressure of passenger numbers, as the English pursue their passion for holiday making.

The upside of the ubiquitous packaged holiday is that the world has become smaller and virtually every destination is accessible. The English make full use of this, possibly more than others. The downside, it seems to me, is that wherever the English go, they are surrounded by others of their own. This is a case of all travel and no knowledge—off the plane and straight down to the beach or the shopping mall, frequently visiting the restaurant that specialises in English food, and two weeks later back home, saying they have been to a foreign country.

Now immigrants who are settled in England are the same, except that when they take their holidays from England they usually fly back to their country of origin, even the ones who have effectively turned their backs on their mother country to live and work abroad. For many, it is a ritual which they feel they have to repeat, year in year out. I know we Asians love to sit and chat, but I question the relaxation benefits. I can see the attraction of keeping in touch with family members whom you have left behind but, for me at least, life has moved on and it is far better to use the benefits of cheap travel to explore the rest of the world. After all, with modern technology, we can speak to and see family members anywhere in the world without leaving our homes, but we have to travel to benefit from experiencing new cultures and enjoying the sights of new locations.

The joy of living in England is that there is no real need to travel abroad. I am quite sure that most people resident here have still not explored everything on offer in England and I would include native Britons here. For a start, there are four different lands within easy reach of one another—England, Scotland, Ireland and Wales. But rather than explore this diversity, the typical English family prefers the annual summer ordeal at the airport to face the horrors of check-in and an excruciatingly uncomfortable flight to some foreign land.

It may simply be that I am writing this as another holiday season approaches, but I am now less inclined than ever to jump on a plane. I may even have made my last trip to India. Unless I treat myself to Upper Class with Virgin Atlantic, relaxing in the Club Lounge, the prospect of sitting in another departure lounge waiting for my delayed flight fills me with dread. I admire the resilience of English travellers, I admire their extraordinary unquestioning patience. Actually, I think the renowned tolerance of the English tourist is beginning to change. Too many of them have travelled the globe and are able to compare with what other airlines and airports have to offer. Everyone has an opinion today and it is no good just putting up a sign apologising for the late departure; people want to know why, what is the alternative, where the free meal vouchers are and, inevitably, what about their compensation?

I am not a tour operator, but I recognise that the opinions of every tourist are easily affected. It does not take much more than a negative story in any country to keep people away. England, and the rest of Britain, suffered from the foot-and-mouth disease outbreak in 2001 and various terrorist outrages did their bit in subsequent years to keep tourist numbers down.

Nevertheless, England remains a prime destination with a steady 4% increase year on year of tourist arrivals. Low cost airlines and the 'open skies' policies between Europe and the United States will all contribute to an increase in visitors.

The type of holiday one took in England used to be based fairly clearly on one's status. For a start, many of the well-off—and for that read upper class—would have enjoyed more than one holiday a year. Winter would have been spent skiing and the summer in some sun-drenched exotic location. Now most people get two holidays a year and everyone who wants to can go skiing and soak up the sun anywhere in the world. The only differentiation is price, and money buys anything, so there is no guarantee you will be able to holiday with the people you normally mix with at home.

So holiday time is a free-for-all, unless, of course, you can gain access to some of the more exclusive islands where entry is by invitation only. There is a certain irony about the fact that Sir Richard Branson, who made his name through cheap travel, bought his own private paradise—Necker Island in the Caribbean—to allow himself and a very select few to escape the rude and scoffing multitude!

What holiday time boils down for the English is a break away from the daily grind, a chance to relax, preferably in a different location with a change of diet. Some 32 million people think England is the ideal place to come and do just that. If you live in England, you could do a lot worse than get out your map and find one of the many corners of England that you have yet to discover.

London alone is the most beautiful and lovable city in the world—in my opinion!

11

A New Era of English Eating and Drinking Habits

Part of the secret of success in life is to eat what you like and let the food fight it out inside.

Mark Twain

Let me say at the outset that I agree the world has gone mad—according to recent statistics, we in England throw away a third of all the food we buy and about 3 million tonnes of that is edible. Despite this fact, over the years, the topsy-turvy world of European food policies has been changed for the better. Now 70% of the European Union's Euro budget actually goes directly to farmers, as opposed to the old ways when 90% was spent on maintaining commodity prices and unwanted food mountains.

But I do not want to dwell on the debates. As the late Dom Helder Camara, the Archbishop of Olinda and Recife, said, 'When I give food to the poor, they call me a saint. When I ask why the poor have no food, they call me a communist.' You cannot win the debate.

It is funny how talk of food can stir up passions. I am passionate about food and in these few pages I will explore what

A New Era of English Eating and Drinking Habits

is on offer on the English table and why it can be so attractive to people wishing to settle in this country.

Let us first deal quickly with curry, which has now overtaken the famous fish and chips as England's most popular meal. As everyone knows, many of the curry dishes originally served and sold in England had little if anything to do with what would be served in India—chicken tikka masala was said to have been invented in Glasgow, but that does not matter. I see it as a gift from India to England, a first step towards mutual understanding, if you like.

Depending on where you live, or dine, the quality of Indian restaurants can be very high and true to the original and you can now expect to find a take-away in every town and even in some smaller villages. The fact that many of these restaurants are packed with Indians enjoying their meals must be a testament to the quality and authenticity of the menu.

The improvement in curries (which did not really exist in England when I first arrived)—even those in supermarkets—is down to the work ethic of the Indian immigrants. The so-called curry kings who arrived in England, quickly realised that what was passing for real Indian cuisine was anything but that, and they set about raising the standards.

Along with our curry, we traditionally drink lager. However, the range of lagers on offer in England was found to be too gassy by one Indian who set up his own factory in England to brew a better product. Cobra beer was a rapid success and its founder, Karan Bilimoria, is now a peer of the realm.

The joy of living in England is that we are at the crossroads of international travel and as such we can enjoy influences from around the world. London probably has good ethnic cuisine from every country, so everyone should be happy.

My own choice is in keeping with my original approach to living in England, so I go for local English dishes which inevitably have been touched by other national cuisines. Roast beef and Yorkshire pudding is, of course, one of the most traditional and original dishes on offer and you have not lived if you have not tasted it at Simpsons-in-the-Strand. I could not really say if that is the best, but it is a classic English dish in a classic English setting. You have to try it at least once.

Now what about those famous fish and chips? The traditional way of eating this is to wrap it in newspaper and soak it in vinegar. Again, it is one of those experiences everyone should have. The better establishments do not overdo the batter around the fish, and the chips should be slightly crisp and dry. I have fond of memories of fish and chips from my early days in England, on a trip to that other icon of England, Stratford-upon-Avon. I have to say that since that time, many decades ago, I have not enjoyed cod and chips of that standard anywhere. Sadly, there is a threat to this business because fish stocks, particularly of cod, are running low, with over-fishing of the seas around us. Some of you may remember the cod wars of the 1950, 1960s and 1970s, with British naval vessels herding away foreign (mainly Icelandic) trawlers, resulting in a number of very close encounters. There is something very English about going to war over a cod.

Fish is a great favourite of mine and if you are feeling adventurous, you should travel to the coast, seek out a small local restaurant and try fish at its freshest. It probably tastes better just because of the anticipation.

Whelks and eels are another typical seaside dish, although they are an acquired taste, which eludes most people, I find. It is said that in England you are never more than about 70 miles from the coast, so it is no surprise that fish plays such an important role in people's diets and in the national psyche.

Even if you do not care for the food, you must surely admire the names like Ploughman's Lunch, Shepherd's Pie, Toad in the Hole—such evocative names of rustic scenes. You can picture the ploughman resting with his hunk of bread, slab of cheese and piece of fruit. If he is lucky, he will have a flask of ale or cider at his side. Yes, all very romanticised I suppose, particularly when you go into some pubs and only get the thinnest slice of processed cheese between two slices of insipid white bread, but when it is done well it is a most satisfying lunch.

A New Era of English Eating and Drinking Habits

While there are some marvellous dishes to be had in England, snack food is the bane of every parent, assuming of course they are not indulging in it themselves—high in fat, sugar and salt and little, if any, nourishment. The result is a young generation turning to fat, even obesity. Child obesity has doubled in recent years, which some medics say is resulting in an increase in Type 2 Diabetes. You can point the finger at America and say their super large portions of chips and fizzy drinks (or as they say, fries and soda) are now being sold here. Even a medium cup of coffee is served in a basin sized tumbler, large enough to bathe in. But you can say no—not an easy word for children, I agree.

Eating for many English people is now simply grazing. People eat and drink while on the move, walking and driving. Some nutritionists argue that eating lightly when you are hungry is the correct way, but I am sure they do not mean munching a Big Mac whenever the urge takes you. It seems as though everything is geared towards eating on the go. Cars have special flask holders for drink bottles and cups of tea and coffee and have you noticed how everyone carries around water bottles with them? Are they suddenly likely to get dehydrated in England's moderate climate? One trend which will inevitably come to England is the American addition of a coffee cup holder to shopping trolleys, meaning you can maintain your caffeine levels even while carrying out regular domestic tasks.

Celebrity chefs, like Jamie Oliver, do their bit to raise standards. He even managed to persuade the government to take the dire state of most school meals seriously, proving on television that it was possible to provide both nourishing and satisfying meals for school children.

It is rare for a week to go by without some new TV series about cooking being launched. The English shows have come a long way from the stylised format of Fanny Craddock and her long suffering husband, Johnnie, back in the 1950s. In fact, Fanny Craddock was a great believer in the influence of French cooking and she gave all her recipes French titles.

Today every chef tries to have their own TV series and from those series you get spin-off competitions to find the next great chef. Gordon Ramsay is probably the most famous name. Although he is a Scot, England can claim him as his fame has been found south of the border! You can enjoy his cuisine at exquisite hotels such as Claridges and the Savoy.

There are those like me who enjoy their food and there are those who find food a nightmare. The most worrying group are probably young girls, like my daughter, who are obsessed with looking thin and eat very little. Taken to its extreme, they become anorexic. The fashion trade has, to a certain extent, accepted some of the blame for this with their insistence on only employing super-thin models. In 2006, there was a move to ban these size zero models from the catwalks. Size zero equates to a 22-inch waistline or the equivalent of an eight-year old's body.

Every day the newspapers invent a new diet launched by some celebrity. It is a terrific way to sell the papers and other merchandise around the diet plan, but fad diets seldom prove a lasting solution to being overweight or even obese. I am not a medic, so I do not intend to give anyone advice about their diets, but eating and drinking a little less of everything usually works for most people. At a book signing a few years ago at Fortnum and Mason, the world famous food and department store at Piccadilly in London, the late Michael Winner, food writer and former Hollywood film maker, was in discussion about a new diet book he was launching. He agreed that sticking to a diet was always difficult and his advice was that you could do a lot worse than just buying smaller plates and eating smaller portions of the food you enjoy.

But back to those who enjoy their food and drink. Climate change, or global warming, is having a remarkable effect on agriculture the world over and England is no exception. Winters are shorter, if a little sharper, the summers are generally longer and drier. All this means that farmers are able to produce increasing amounts of Mediterranean-style crops and one of the most significant impacts has been on the English vineyards.

Initially, English wine was regarded as a bit of a joke, expensive and not much to write home about. But all this is changing. Wine production has slowly been increasing and 2006 was a bumper year with production up to three million bottles. Apparently sparkling wine was doing particularly well. The Nyetimber Classic Cuvée 1998 from West Sussex was declared the best sparkling wine in the world outside the French Champagne Region, in 2006. That could set you back quite a bit financially, should you be interested in trying some! I suppose the ultimate accolade is the fact that French shops, particularly those in the booze-cruise destinations like Calais, are actually selling English wines.

But is all this so new? According to historical records, the English were cultivating vineyards in Britain 2,000 years ago, when the climate was much milder in the so-called Roman Warming period. According to the RealClimate.com website, Domesday Book records show more than 40 vineyards in southern England. This might suggest that climate change is cyclical as well as human-made, but that is not a topic of debate for this book.

We should also consider the enormous expansion of organic food cultivation. People are rightly concerned about their health, and therefore of what they are eating. This concern has been picked up quickly by the supermarkets and independent food retailers. Traditionally, if you wanted a real potato covered in earth to prove its provenance, you had to go to your local greengrocer, who probably also knew the farmer who delivered it, but now you find more and more shelves in supermarkets promoting organic food.

It is probably true to say that genuinely organic food is better for you than the mass-produced alternatives sprayed with pesticides and other chemicals. But for every article praising organic food, there is another talking about the marketing con-job, challenging the claims to be completely pesticide free and even warning of the hazards of eating untreated food. Clearly, food is a topic that is never far from the English mind and is a classic topic of conversation.

Nevertheless, the demand for organic food is undeniable and it seems customers are not put off by the high cost of most organic food. There is an irony though when one recognises that supermarkets are having to import increasing amounts of organic produce to meet the demand. People have got used to eating what they want, when they want, regardless of the season. Flying in food from around the world is hardly a green policy. There is an additional worry that because English farmers cannot meet domestic demand, foreign imports have to make up the difference and strict UK/English food quality standards may not apply elsewhere.

The rules and regulations for farmers to comply with are stringent and many find the paperwork involved makes the whole process unviable. In other words, they are spending more time filling in forms than they are actually out on their tractors, managing their crops. A third of organic farmers in England are not making money.

So how many of us are eating organic food? The latest statistics said organic food sales had risen 30%, undoubtedly a big increase, but that still only represented 1.3% of the total annual food and drink market. Despite the hype, there are signs that the growth, at least in the demand for organic food, is slowing.

It is possible that this desire to eat properly and well is having a beneficial spin-off effect for small towns and villages. Some areas are reporting a significant increase in farmers' markets—these are traditional markets with stalls and local produce on sale. These markets are usually held once a week and are always popular. They also give a major boost to smaller towns, which have seen many of their traditional shops like butchers and greengrocers, forced out of business by large supermarkets.

In the end, of course, it comes down to convenience and confidence. Supermarkets are under constant pressure to maintain very high standards and, by and large, their food must be safe, otherwise they cannot survive and prosper. Also, people like the convenience and the price. The supermarket is always there, not just once a week, and is open long hours.

A New Era of English Eating and Drinking Habits

Lastly, I would like to sing the praises of the traditional English tea. I am an unashamed fan of this institution and from time to time I indulge myself with tea at the Ritz, another exquisite hotel, with all its glamour and china, and beautifully prepared cucumber sandwiches and delicious cakes. At these sorts of places, the English have turned taking tea into an art form. Again, I would recommend it to everyone to try at least once.

Tea is another gift from India, as well as China of course, but somehow the English have made it their own. Traditionally, afternoon tea is served at 4 p.m. and in some of the grander houses and many hotels, everything stops for tea. Although it is a stimulant, the English will serve it in times of stress and upset, 'Have a nice cup of tea, dear, it will calm you down.' It probably will not, but there is definitely something soothing about it. Maybe it is the process of having to stop, sit still and drink that calms the nerves. The ancients would claim it has a medicinal value, probably mostly with the so-called infusions.

I suppose what I like about it most is that the whole process of taking tea has developed into a civilised practice. While its origins are undoubtedly from the Eastern world, my beloved England has infused it with style and panache and raised it to a level unmatched in any other country!

12

The English National Health and Welfare

> Do not believe yourself healthy. Immortality is health; this life is a long sickness.
>
> St Augustine

When Aneurin Bevan pushed through his bill in the Westminster Parliament on 5th July 1948 creating the National Health Service (the NHS), he could not have imagined the monster he had conceived. It is the largest employer in Europe, with a staff in England of some 1.3 million and commands a budget of £101.3 billion in England (2015 figures). Combined with all the benefits provided by the country's social services, the total health and welfare package on offer in England is a staggering gift to those who accept it.

For those who are not aware, the NHS provides free care at the point of delivery, paid for in the main out of taxes. The downside of this benevolence is that there is a huge demand on its services and queues, or waiting lists, build up for minor and serious treatments. To get around these delays, those who can afford it, go private. This is usually paid for out of insurance policies and subscriptions to healthcare providers like BUPA and PPP.

In fact, a majority of doctors were opposed to the establishment of the NHS, fearing that they would lose out on their lucrative private practice. However, when it was introduced, 95% of the medical practitioners joined the NHS and today there is a workable system for consultants and doctors to divide their time between public and private practice.

In recent years, changes in the NHS have resulted in an increasing role for the private sector which has become involved in supplying a number of services and funding some buildings, including new hospitals. Although the ultimate authority lies with the Department of Health, more and more key decisions are being taken at the local level. This does mean that there can be quite significant differences between countries within the United Kingdom; for example, a recent law abolished prescription charges for medicines in Wales, while on the same day in April 2007 the charges increased in England.

Funding has always been at the root of the trouble. One thing in common between the early NHS and its modern equivalent is that financial estimates were wildly out then and continue to be today; it was estimated that the NHS would be costing about £150 million by 1950, in fact the figure was nearer £350 million. The NHS was short of money then and it is short of money now. Clearly, things could not go on like this and the first prescription charges were introduced in 1951. Bevan resigned; his vision had been a free service for all and to this day, English people's passions are aroused when there is talk of privatising the NHS. It came as no surprise when Danny Boyle's staggeringly original opening ceremony for the 2012 London Olympics featured a tribute to the doctors and nurses of the NHS—a gesture which reflected the true love of the English for their health service.

Seen from the outside, all this free health, free support, and often free housing looks all too tempting, and it is. Undoubtedly, there are scroungers working the system and there are also genuine refugees like the Asians thrown out of Uganda in 1972 and, more recently, those fleeing persecution and the troubles in Eastern Europe and the Middle East. But few would argue that there are thousands of people just taking advantage of social welfare benefits—some of the long-term unemployed for example. There are gaping loopholes in the borderless and ever-growing European Union. Even the decision of the United Kingdom to leave the EU is not likely to affect the free movement of people throughout Europe. But I will leave that debate to others and restrict myself to describing a health and welfare system of such unbounded generosity that few in need would be left out of it.

England is full of contradictions about its population's health. We are certainly all living longer, partly because of better diets, more health awareness and finer medicine; the hospitals will use every piece of new technology to keep the elderly and the tiny premature baby alive, whereas in the past they would have certainly died. Yet, we are told that most adults in England are overweight and some 8 million, or one in 5, are obese. The reasons, we are told, are that we lead an increasingly sedentary lifestyle and are not eating properly. How strange that everywhere you look there is a new fitness centre opening and yet out on the street children are waddling around like bloated little whales.

Like everything else in life, it comes down to examples set by elders. If your parents are overweight, there is a good chance that you, too, will be overweight. In the same way, if your parents are smokers, it is highly like that you, too, will smoke. Why not, if that is the example your elders and supposedly betters are setting? The problem is, of course, that it is these people who are putting further stresses and strains on the NHS and on the social services. The downward spiral is rapid; soon the individual becomes too obese to hold down a job, but he or she still needs food and drink. Then, as the obesity increases, because they are not getting out and about, diabetes kicks in and they are in need of medical help.

In August 2006, the then Health Secretary, Patricia Hewitt, said, 'The Government's got a responsibility to make it easier for people to make healthy choices for themselves.' Some call this sort of statement 'the nanny state gone mad'—why do people need to be helped to do the right thing to help themselves?

But this is the England I love. I am talking about it as I do not want to paint a picture of streets full of blubber. Happily, people in England do live longer than they used to and on the whole it is a lifestyle that most enjoy. England is a centre for medical research and pioneering work is carried out here in some of our great hospitals. It is often down to the skill of the professionals that keeps many alive when in the past they would surely have died.

Headline writers make much of the problems—hospital superbugs, outbreaks of legionnaire's disease, the lack of NHS dentists and so on, but life cannot be that bad or else why would people be flocking to England in droves? Whether England can absorb so many is a subject for debate. I imagine a poll would say: Stop! We are full up! This was certainly an argument put forward by many supporters of the EU exit campaign run ahead of the 2016 referendum to decide whether the United Kingdom should remain a member of the EU.

I read an interesting piece by Sarah Cleghorn, the American poet and social reformer, who died in 1959. She said, 'I wish more and more that health was studied half as much as disease is. Why, with all the endowment of research against cancer, is no study made of those who are free from cancer? Why not inquire what foods they eat, what habits of body and mind they cultivate? And why never study animals in healthy and natural surroundings? Why always sickened and in an environment of strangeness and artificiality?'

She makes a valid point and one thing we can study is the lifestyle of the different races and ethnic groups coming to England. The diet of many English people has changed in large part because of the new styles of cooking which immigrants have introduced. There is a huge demand for the various styles of yoga and probably every city in the land has some form of martial arts club.

So while the couch potatoes may be on the increase, so are the health conscious. Smoking is banned in almost all public places and a similar message will go through about sensible eating and drinking. A tax has been introduced on adding sugar to manufactured food and drink and in recent years, food manufacturers have taken steps to reduce the salt content of many popular products.

Healthy living, food fads and celebrity diets are lucrative territory for the stars of today. It seems everyone is promoting the latest, best system for losing weight. These systems come and go, but if the net effect is for people to be more concerned about their health then, on balance, they are a good thing. In fact, I have some sympathy with George Dennison Prentice, the American 19th century writer who said, 'What some call health, if purchased by perpetual anxiety about diet, isn't much better than tedious disease.' The fads of today are indeed becoming tiresome. It is almost impossible to go out for a meal without somebody saying they do not eat this or that, or insisting on some complicated alternative without salt or without caffeine or, it seems to me, without any pleasurable taste at all. To be frank, I think it is verging on bad manners, particularly if the host and hostess have gone to great lengths to prepare a meal, only for the guests to say their diet will not allow them to eat one particular dish or another. Better not accept any invitation at all while you are enduring that sort of restrictions than to inflict such regimen on others.

I do not recall any such preoccupation with healthy living in the media when I first arrived in England. For most people, it was a time for rebuilding after the austerity of the war years—obesity certainly was not a problem. Food was mainly stodgy and principally designed to fill the gaps—at least that was what was on the mind of this young articled clerk. Nor did people concern themselves with pollution. People were all smoking like chimneys and the factory chimneys were belching out smoke too, as industry met the demands to rebuild the nation's assets.

Someone reading these words in, say, India where boom times are in full flow, might not agree with such a concern for health. Indians, and for that matter the Chinese as well as the developing countries, all want the economic prosperity that the West has enjoyed for so long. So what if there is a little, even a lot, of pollution? The factories are working to capacity and when we can afford it, we will consider other matters like health.

The English and people like me who have come to live permanently in England do, it has to be said, take such things as the NHS for granted. Somehow, it seems that it has always been there and will continue to be there when we turn up at Accident and Emergency at the dead of night and expect a highly trained doctor or nurse to be ready and waiting. They can be waiting, but we cannot be kept waiting. Long may those young doctors and nurses stick to their professional calling, because calling is what it is. The hours are long and ill-rewarded. Often, the midnight customers they have to face are drunk and abusive and still these doctors keep coming through the medical schools. They also keep coming from abroad to fill the gaps, because the gaps keep appearing.

There is also a certain irony about the development of the so-called health tourism, where patients decide to skip the queues and fly abroad—often to India—where they are welcomed into five-star luxury hospitals, operated on and they return home as though they have been on an extravagant holiday. This quick fix is not without its critics who warn that complications after operations occasionally occur and if you are back in Blighty after receiving treatment in Mumbai, there is no aftercare service.

So I suppose we are left with a delightful conundrum—why are so many people rushing to England to enjoy all its wonders of free health and free welfare, provided by so many immigrant nurses and doctors from the likes of India and the Philippines, while so many living here are rushing to those very countries looking for a quick health fix? Some, to be fair, are in too much pain to spend another day on a waiting list, while others are just too impatient.

For myself, I cannot say I have ever been on a diet, although I probably should lose a bit—who shouldn't? I do not avoid any particular food and I enjoy a drink or two. Mark Twain gave us the guide here, 'Water, taken in moderation, cannot hurt anybody.'

St Augustine's words at the start of this chapter are really too gloomy if taken at face value. I would rather take life as it comes and try and meet the blows and rewards with equanimity and a smile on my face. Mind you, as I take this approach, it is good to know that in England the health services, both public and private, are there to help when I am dealt any blows to my health—for which I shall always be grateful to England my love!

Receiving Award from Dr. Shashi Tharoor

13

England's Treasure: The Countryside

Nor rural sights alone, but rural sounds,
Exhilarate the spirit, and restore
The tone of languid Nature.

The Task, William Cowper

For the first few years of my life in England, it took a while for me to appreciate the full beauty of the English countryside, stuck as I was in the grim cityscapes of Manchester and Birmingham. Even now, some 60 years on, I have hardly scratched the surface. Actually, for the purposes of this chapter, I should consider the whole of the British Isles. There can be few islands of this size with such a breadth of landscape, from the Highlands of Scotland to the gentle slopes of the southern counties of England.

Initially, for me, England amounted to towns and cities with little opportunity to explore beyond. In fact, it seemed to me at the time that I had swapped one block of concrete in Delhi and Calcutta, which were at least warm, for another in England, which was not! Now in my later years, I live just outside London with all the garden I can manage or indeed need. But I would like to explore in the next few pages the treasures to be found in England's green and pleasant land, and in the rest of the British Isles, too.

If any visitor to England has time, they could do a lot worse than take a train ride from north to south and watch the changes of the countryside unfold before them. In the space of just a few hours, the transformation would astound them.

But we can also take an instant aerial view of the islands, which have been twisted and carved through gigantic earth movements over 3,000 million years ago. Essentially, the mighty highlands of Scotland were thrown up by great movements in the earth's crust and convulsive outpourings of molten rock. The land twisted and turned, almost tipping over it seemed, and at times plunging what we know as Southern England under water, only for it to rise again. Indeed, the Thames Valley was the last part of the country to emerge from the waters about 15 million years ago, in a subterranean event which also raised the Alps.

So stretching down from the Scottish mountains, you have the rugged Pennines, then the Hill Country, which is a line of limestone and sandstone hills running from the North Yorkshire moors through the Cotswolds all the way down to Dorset. Then you have the lowlands to the east and south. If you arrive by boat on the south coast, you will be greeted by the famous White Cliffs of Dover. Three times in the last 180 million years these lowlands of England were submerged, leaving the deposits of chalk as well as clay and limestone, which we see today.

It was in these fertile lowlands where most of the earliest settlements occurred. Today Kent and Sussex are the heart of the Garden of England—and, if the housing prices are anything to go by, the most popular counties in which to live and work in England. This is where you find the hop gardens where beer used to start its life. Oast houses were used to dry the hops, which were spread on the floors with a fire burning beneath. The heat rose through perforations in the floor and escaped through wooden cowls, which turned in the wind. Modern industrial methods are now used to dry the hops, although many old oast houses have been preserved or converted into homes. But I must not allow the delights of English ales to side-track me from the tour!

England's Treasure: The Countryside

Whenever I think of the English countryside, I think of trees. Before the Ice Age 10,000 years ago, much of the land was covered with trees and today there are some 1,300 different species, the most famous of all being the mighty oak. The oldest English trees are yews, which can survive almost 2,000 years, while the average life of an oak is more like 500 years.

A lot of English history seems to be linked to these trees—the great fleets which set out across the high seas exploring and conquering were hewn from these timbers. The Victorian traders and empire builders were enlightened enough to send back countless different specimens from the far flung worlds they discovered on their voyages. The yew was the wood of choice for the long bow, more than six feet high, and the real star of battles like Agincourt (1415), when Henry V took on and defeated the army of Charles VI of France. And, more recently, where would English cricket be without the willow—the traditional wood used to make cricket bats?

If we take to the air once more in the south, we can see the patchwork quilt of fields bounded by hedgerows, ditches and dry stonewalls. Even though the life is tough and, for most, hardly rewarding, farmers are the custodians of the landscape. There is little arable land and the pasture is enclosed with stone walls. Elsewhere there are hedgerows and ditches dividing the landscape into small parcels of land.

This enclosure farming is relatively recent in the grand scheme of things, beginning in the mid-18th century when landowners saw potential profit in farming and began to work their land more intensely and efficiently. Unfortunately, this was not good news for the villagers who were dispossessed as the hitherto large open spaces were suddenly divided up.

More recently, fields became bigger as hedges were grubbed out. This was all to do with the economics of farming and using more modern equipment. Too many hedges and stone wall boundaries meant the farmers lost acreage. In the nick of time, it was realised that this was detrimental to the countryside, not the least to wildlife which relied on the hedges for nesting, cover and shelter. Campaigns were started and farmers can now get grants to reinstate and re-lay hedges and rebuild stone walls, all of which are increasingly forgotten arts. You do not just rebuild a stone wall by putting one old rock on top of another. It can take many years to learn the intricate techniques of building stable and long-lasting walls, and thankfully, this is one of the many rural skills that has in recent years seen a revival of interest.

I suppose everyone's ideal is to live in the country, near a village, but with easy access to a big town. These places do exist, but are quickly snapped up when they come on the market. Possibly the next best thing is actually to live in a quiet village steeped in history.

The archetypal village setting is one with a church at its centre, with a green or pond, surrounded by cottages, with some local shops. Occasionally there will be a cricket pitch, where matches are played at a leisurely pace, or bowling greens where, I am sure, beneath the genteel surface, the battles are in deadly earnest.

It is a great struggle for these villages to retain their facilities and villagers fight fierce campaigns to keep their local post office alive and their local stores, but the harsh economic realities of life make it difficult for them to survive. Interestingly, it is the entrepreneurial spirit of the Asian community and they are increasingly stepping into the breach when local shops become available. Somehow they seem to be able to breathe new life into the stores.

Historically, villages grew from the open field system of farming as local communities developed around the land. You will not find them now, but originally there would have been a forge to shoe the horses who worked the fields. Nowadays mobile farriers travel the country, lighting up their instant forges as they move from stable yard to stable yard. Then, general stores would have arrived, providing every conceivable product. The church would have been the centre of life, probably attended by most of the villagers. Not far away there would be a pub or sometimes an old coaching inn, where weary travellers would rest themselves and their horses as they made their way across the country in days of yore. These villages often have winding roads running through them and tiny lanes. By contrast, you also have street villages with houses built on either side of a main road, with lines of homes often running east to west so all inhabitants got some sunlight.

Fishing villages were simply developed where there was a suitable bit of beach to land the boats or a sheltered cove to create a harbour. You can find these all along the coast and they retain a unique charm. In places like Cornwall, down on the south western-most tip of England, fish restaurants have become major attractions in their own right.

This brings me back to the very individual and distinctive coastline of England—gentle sandy beaches—of nearly 5,000 km, surrounded by a myriad of islands such as the Isle of Wight and the Isle of Man.

The call of the sea is irresistible for many of the English, and this has had an impact on the look and feel of seaside towns and villages. The National Trust, an independent charity which works to preserve and protect the countryside and old buildings of England, Wales and Northern Ireland, is worried about the urban sprawl along the coastline. The Trust fears that many coastal areas will be endangered unless town planners take greater care. Of course, it is not just humans at fault, nature is also at play here, carving away at the beaches, threatening whole communities with flooding. Around 2 million properties in England and Wales are located in flood risk areas. It seems the only certainty is that flooding will continue to occur regardless of flood defences. The only other certainty is that people are prepared to take that risk, because the demand for housing in the south, in particular, is relentless.

So the countryside and nature are both beauties to behold and yet awesome in their destructive power. England is blessed with a rich landscape, full of variety, and that variety is matched by the changing seasons.

One of the enormous attractions of England is surprisingly the fact that you get winter months along with spring, summer and autumn. I regard it as a benefit of global warming that the English climate is generally becoming milder. This will have an impact on the countryside, but the changes are unlikely to be so severe that England will lose the changing seasons.

If I am honest, I cannot say that when I first arrived here, I had all this in mind. I suppose, as a young boy, I would not have enjoyed the cold, rain and snow, but I am in no doubt that the seasons make the English countryside and I am certain no-one could ever tire of travelling through this land and appreciating how it all evolved.

There are always surprises waiting around the corner. Let me leave this topic by giving you one example. I was a little early for a weekend pint in a village I was passing through. The pub had not opened, because 24-hour drinking had not reached this quiet corner, and probably never would. Inevitably, there was a local church nearby, so out of curiosity I wandered through the lych-gate and strolled through the graveyard, admiring the ancient stones. An elderly lady was raking up some sticks and leaves and paused to welcome me. It seems she and her parents before her, had volunteered to keep the gardens tidy. She told me the wonderful history of the church, how it had altered over the years and, of course, she knew everything about the village, where she had lived most of her life.

To me, this moment somehow encapsulated everything that was typical of a true rural community. It is possible to escape to these little idylls all over the country, if we only make the effort, and occasionally we can get lucky and find someone who is only too happy to pass on their stories. We can, of course, spend our holiday jetting off to a beach somewhere, but I doubt whether we would find the same real satisfaction as we would from a long weekend pottering among these forgotten treasures.

I said my goodbyes to my elderly guide and I enjoyed my pint in the English sun even more.

14

The English Passion for Animals

All animals are equal, but some animals are more equal than others.

Animal Farm, George Orwell

The English are a nation of animal lovers and yet they hunt them, shoot them and fish for them like no other people. To the English, there is nothing contradictory about that statement, in fact they would argue that the continued practice of hunting in all its forms confirms their love for animals.

So much of what we love about the English countryside—the copses, woodlands and hedges—is there as a direct result of this love of hunting. Copses were created and preserved specifically to create places for foxes to breed. Pheasant, about as English as you can get in the traditional picture postcard scene, but actually originally from India, are reared in land preserved for them. The moorlands are maintained for the grouse shoots and the English passion for shooting is reflected in the name given to 12th August, on which the annual grouse shooting season begins, The Glorious Twelfth.

When fox hunting was banned by Parliament, two typically idiosyncratic English events happened—membership of foxhunts increased dramatically along with the 'fields' that turned out on horseback or on foot throughout the hunting season, and it appears that more foxes were killed. The explanation for the increased number of kills, I think, remains a mystery to all. As for the increased number of hunt supporters, I suspect that was almost entirely down to the fact that when the English are told they cannot do something, they immediately go out and do it. That attitude even extended to people who had no interest in hunting, until the ban was introduced. The widely held opinion was, 'I don't particularly care for hunting, but I will defend to my last breath the right of an individual to do so.' There was rioting in Parliament Square on the night of the vote, when passions were running high among normally quiet, law abiding citizens—the so-called green welly brigade, the well-to-do rural middle classes, are not easily stirred—and the House of Commons Chamber itself was invaded briefly by protestors.

I am not taking sides with the pro-hunting lobby or the Antis, as they are called, just reporting the facts as I see them. It seems to me that we will never be able to reconcile the two camps. You either believe it is entirely wrong to kill another creature or you do not. Of course, left to their own devices, the fox population would grow uncontrollably. It seems to me that some form of culling is essential for the long term good of the herds.

Organised pheasant, grouse and partridge shoots do appear to be something of a slaughter and, to my way of thinking, it is not a terribly pleasant spectacle to see rows and rows of dead birds behind a line of smoking guns. The tragedy of these events is that they are increasingly laid on for corporate days or for tourists and I believe that many shoots simply bury most of the birds afterwards. Some of these large estates are faced with ever increasing costs and if they have to turn to the tourist trade to boost their income, then that is what will happen. At least in recent years, there has been an increase in England in the consumption of game produce such as venison, so I would hope that some of those poor creatures have not died in vain.

Despite this fondness for hunting—and I would include a sport like fishing which has a huge following throughout the country—I sometimes think the English love their animals more than their fellow human beings. They cannot stand suffering and the RSPCA (Royal Society for the Prevention of Cruelty to Animals) is a large organisation, ready to investigate anyone suspected of causing an animal any suffering.

Let us move away from hunting and examine the English affinity towards animals. They say a 'man's best friend' is the dog and that certainly applies to many English households, where it is commonplace to find at least one dog. The most famous dog show in the world—the annual Crufts event organised by the Kennel Club—is held in the UK and attracts 6,000 visitors every year, with millions more watching on television. In the countryside, not necessarily on farms, some families will have more than one dog, a cat or two and possibly horses.

Horse riding is one of the most popular sporting activities and there are about a million or more horses and ponies around the English countryside. When they are not just hacking out around the roads or bridleways, the owners will be hunting or competing at various shows and gymkhanas. The horses have to be fed and watered daily and if they live in stables they have to be mucked out every day and there are constant shoeing and veterinary requirements. Keeping a horse is a very time consuming hobby and yet there are plenty of people who would prefer to be out in their yards messing about with their horses than anywhere else.

The famous reserve of the English only melts when faced with an animal. 'No hugging, dear. I'm English. We only show affection to dogs and horses,' is a delightful and apt quote from the film *What a Girl Wants*, when a young girl attempts to hug a particularly staid, older woman. The continental style embrace with a kiss on both cheeks has, though, caught on in recent years much to the discomfort of anyone over 50 and probably to the delight of men like me who are over 70!

So are animals an obsession with the English? They may not consider it an obsession but many would feel their home is somehow incomplete without an animal. Do not be surprised when you go to an English home and see a dog curled up on a chair. For that matter, do not be surprised to hear that some people let their small dogs sleep on their beds. The huge damp elk hound steaming happily by a grand open fire is a rarer sight, simply because the grand old homes no longer exist, converted as so many of them have been into hotels, but in traditional country family homes, the dog is king.

Having said that, I also observe that changes are occurring in the English attitude to animals and it is disrupting the normal way of life when people could be easily divided into those who lived in the country and those who lived in towns. Traditionally, country dwellers all had animals and those in towns often did not, apart from the odd cat. But increasing numbers of newly rich people are moving out of English towns into smart and stylish properties where, sadly, there is no room for an animal of any sort. There are a number of reasons for this. First and foremost, having an animal cramps their lifestyle. No one is prepared to have a muddy dog jumping around on their pristine furniture nor do they want the cat leaving its hair on the carpets. Also, no one is prepared to spend time exercising the dog. On some of the grander and newer estates, where the lawns are manicured to perfection, there is nowhere for a dog to run free, anyway.

Such sanitised living, surprisingly, can have its down side, too. It appears there has been a dramatic increase in Type 1 diabetes among very young children and there is some evidence to say this is caused by families living in germ free bubbles, as germ and dust-free also means no ventilation and no build-up of immunities. Professor Polly Bingley, from the University of Bristol, said that the increase, 'must be due to changes in our environment. This could either mean that we are being exposed to something new, or that we now have reduced exposure to something that was previously controlling our immune responses.' A bit of dirt never hurt anyone, English grandmothers used to say.

The migration to the countryside by affluent town dwellers is something which can cause local upset. The townies like the look of the country—all the trees and hedges and grass—but they do not like the messy bits. So what happens when someone who has made their fortune buys themselves a large house in the country? The first thing they do is tear down the hedge surrounding the house and put up a high wooden fence to protect their privacy. Of course, what they are also doing is destroying nesting places for birds and blocking off runs for foxes and deer. They are, in effect, gradually destroying the very reason why they chose to live in the countryside.

Perhaps England itself is changing. There is a pretence towards a love of animals—the odd fish pond in the garden or a couple of guinea pigs for the children—but can people be bothered with the responsibilities of looking after anything more demanding than these modest creatures? The growth business for vets is small animals—low maintenance for the owners. I have looked at what is happening to the countryside in the previous chapter, but the migration of wealthy people, whose natural habitat is the town, into the country is definitely creating a clash of cultures.

My English friends tell me that the traditional country folk are in retreat. Their rides through once quiet country lanes are threatened by the fast and noisy sports car of the celebrity who has moved into the 'big house'. What is emerging from the new country residents is a combination of ignorance about other people and creatures using the roads—badgers, foxes, deer and cats—and the lack of courtesy and respect which I have mentioned elsewhere.

At the same time, new affluence arriving in a village is not altogether negative. There is no doubt that many a Pony Club is enjoying revitalised activity—more than 35,000 members at the last count and rising—as the demand for a bigger and better ponies grows louder from youngsters who are aiming to win rosettes. In fact, that is where the difference between the new and old order gets defined. In the past, the parents and grandparents of country children may well have ridden horses themselves. The newcomers from the towns now arrive at a horse show in a spanking new horse box or trailer, but parents would not be interested the proceedings and would be counting the minutes, until it was time to scoop up their child and leave. If you like, it is a token nod in the direction of country pursuits, but there is no real desire to get too involved.

I doubt whether there is any other race with quite such a regard for animals as the English. I should make a special mention of horse racing which, of course, is an international sport, but from an outsider's point of view, somehow England is regarded as the place to win. There are so many English races and race meetings which have an aura about them which somehow others lack—Royal Ascot, the Grand National, the Cheltenham Gold Cup, the Derby—the list goes on and these meetings have a history which dates back generations. Top hat and tails for the men and glamorous dresses and hats for the women are *de rigeur* in the Royal Enclosure at Ascot. Where else would you enjoy such pomp and ceremony?

Mystery and drama also surround horse racing, the so-called sport of kings. Even if you are not a race goer, you may well have heard of Devon Loch, the Queen Mother's horse, which was just 45 metres from the winning post in the 1956 Grand National and appeared to jump a jump which was not there and fell. Or the stallion, Shergar, who won the 1981 Epsom Derby by a record 10 lengths only to become even more famous two years later when he was kidnapped from a stud in County Kildare, Ireland, never to be seen again. Most people believe he was snatched by the IRA, who killed him after a £2 million ransom demand failed.

After he retired from the saddle, one of the most popular jockeys of all time, Dick Francis, went on to write countless novels based in and around the world of horse racing, and became a globally famous, best-selling author. It seems that even if people do not want to participate in the sport, they are eager to read about it.

The debate about hunting was hostile enough territory upon which to tread. The multi-faith nation that England has become presents a whole of host of different attitudes towards animals. Some people are positively repelled even by the touch of a dog—I have witnessed this on the Tube in London when someone's dog just brushed against another passenger's leg. Nothing was said but the reaction to move away from the animal was immediate. By contrast, the English have annual services in some churches to bless all the animals—the smaller ones are even carried to the church.

Of course, the English are not unique in their affection towards animals, nor indeed in their religious belief in recognising the importance of animals in this world. Many religions also preach respect for animals, but the English seem to carry it a step further, sometimes even to the point of eccentricity. They are invariably blind to their pets' obvious faults and will spare no expense to keep them well. Again, the boom time which veterinary clinics in the country are enjoying is testimony to the fact that the English will do anything to keep their pets well.

Such sentimentality is coupled with realism—farm animals are bred to be eaten. Their owners may well give their cows and pigs pet names, but when their time is up, they are off to the slaughter house, only for a new batch to arrive and to be treated with the same kindness.

I would place a small bet that the dream of most English people is to live in the country, with a little bit of land and a dog. Despite all the changes to lifestyle and background, the saying still holds good, 'love me, love my dog.'

With British High Commissioner to India

15

Where Would the English be without the Weather?

Mad Dogs and Englishmen go out in the midday sun.

Noel Coward

Surely there is no better way to start a conversation with an Englishman or lady than by discussing the weather. Traditionally, this has been their opening remark when introduced to a guest at a social gathering. 'What terrible weather we are having,' or, 'What a glorious day,' are often heard at the start of a conversation. You are on safe ground, because you are not asking questions about the other person's personal or business life; the English natural reserve is not under threat.

Of course, things have changed in recent years with the upheaval in climate and the large changes, but I will come to global warming a little later. For now, we are looking at the first impressions of an immigrant arriving in England at the end of the 1950s. Although the weather happened to be fine on the particular day I arrived, the whole world knew that England was famous for its rain and its umbrellas.

I am greatly indebted to Tom Quinn and his wonderful book, *Tales of the Country Eccentrics*, for the story about one Colonel Alfred

Daniel Wintle who was so fond of his umbrella that he took it to bed with him. According to Wintle, knowledge of umbrellas and a proper regard for them was the true mark of the English. Apparently he said, 'No Englishman ever unfurls his umbrella, which means he gets wet.' There was a time when a true gentleman could be judged by how tightly his brolly was furled.

The elegant umbrella with its wooden handle, of course, has now been somewhat replaced by the large and gaily coloured golfing umbrellas, often sporting some form of advertising or logo, which people use nowadays in the cities as well as on the golf links, making it virtually impossible to walk down the street in the rain without risk of losing an eye.

The English speak constantly about the weather and yet seem impervious to it. Hot or cold, wet or dry, the English traditionally take what the elements throw at them and continue much the same. Noel Coward was right about the English, particularly when travelling abroad. But when at home, despite this masterly *sang froid* approach to everything, they never seem prepared for the extremes when they hit them.

The prime example is, of course, the snow. It always catches the English by surprise now and even when I first arrived. Trains slither to a halt and traffic jams pile up on motorways, whether or not the gritting lorries have been out doing their stuff. The problem, no doubt, is that there is never enough snow to make proper provision for it. In Canada, they would expect to see several feet of snow every year and everyone copes, the roads are clear and transport runs normally. But in the British Isles, and especially my beloved England, there is never enough to bother with; when it arrives for a few days, schools take extra holidays, the transport stops for a time, TV and radio news channels go into overtime about it and then it is all back to normal.

Just as the cold snaps take the English by surprise every year, so do the hot spells and subsequent droughts. Actually, it is one of the delights in England when the sun suddenly bursts forth but, once again, the country has a tendency to overdo the reaction. Every square inch of green grass in the London parks is covered with sunbathers during their lunch breaks, all determined to top up their tans—or, more likely, get burnt like so many lobsters.

And you can be quite sure that the transport will again be affected—tarmac on the roads will begin to melt, rails will buckle and the underground system in London will struggle to cope, leaving the poor, unfortunate commuters sweltering in the carriages. This does provide an opportunity to watch the peculiarly English character at work. Crammed cheek by jowl, all eye contact will be avoided, not a word will be spoken to one's neighbour perhaps less than a few inches away, all sweating profusely. The great English stoicism, the ability to put up with extraordinary discomfort and inconvenience with scarcely more than a murmur of complaint, is a wonder to behold.

Having said that, it is traditional to complain about the rail services running into London and the other major cities, the point is that these services are being stretched to breaking point, year by year.

But back to the weather. It is a truism that weather has a bearing on a nation's character. In the warm, Latin countries there is more *joie de vivre*, more spontaneity, more passion. In the chillier northern climes like England, the tendency to wrap up against the elements is reflected in the more reserved and introverted character. A common saying, which is so characteristic of the English stoicism is, 'There is no such thing as bad weather, only inappropriate clothing.' But like a flower which blooms all too briefly when the sun hits it, I have noticed that the English are changing.

This brings me to climate change and global warming. The warmer winters and hotter summers England is experiencing, particularly in the south, are having an impact on the traditional way of life.

Let me give a few examples. The street cafés, which are springing up everywhere, are trying to copy the Parisian boulevards and Italian piazzas. At first, it was the tentative table and chair outside a café and everyone smirked at the few hardy individuals who sat out, probably breathing in more petrol fumes than roasted coffee beans. But gradually the trend caught on, helped by the increasing pedestrianisation of many city streets. On warm summer evenings in some restaurants, there are more people sitting outside than inside.

Then, of course, air conditioning arrived. When I first came to this country, it was virtually unheard of. Today, every modern car has AC, every new restaurant has it and all new apartment buildings at the top end of the price range offer it as standard. This is not just for fun or as a status symbol, it is a reflection of the changing climate.

As there is such a noisy debate about global warming, I think I should touch on it briefly, particularly as England is taking a lead role in much of the argument. Essentially, there are two camps—those who believe humans are the culprits and those who believe the human input into the equation is insignificant. The English are fundamentally a fair race and they would not want to hold back any developing nation such as India or China from catching with up the developed western world in economic and industrial performance. So they commissioned serious studies, like the Stern Report, which looked at the economic impact of global warming. Its message was, it is not too late but we must start doing something about it.

Typically, there was an immediate contrarian view published in *The Sunday Telegraph*, casting doubt on the various statistics and evidence for the case of human-caused global warming. Then other dissenting voices spoke up; the human impact on the production of $CO2$ is insignificant compared with the impact the sun has on the world's temperature and as for melting ice caps—well it seems they melt and grow all the time.

I mention all this because it has some bearing on the English character. The English do not like being told what is good for them by people in authority. Indeed, the English have a fundamental suspicion of anyone in authority. So tell an English person that they cannot do something or they should start doing something else and their immediate reaction is to do precisely the opposite.

Personally, I have no idea whether global warming, or 'climate change' as it is euphemistically called, is entirely caused by humans or whether we are just in one of those cycles of nature, probably being helped along by people's disregard for pollution and the environment. What I do like is the effect the warmer weather is having on the English. I like the street cafés, I like the more relaxed, and dare I say it, continental style, that has been adopted here. It is as though we are enjoying the best of all possible worlds.

One of the great English traditions in recent years is to jump on the ferry to France on a so called booze cruise, fill the car up with low priced wine and beer, have a good day out and return home. The English are consummate travellers and they are ready to adopt the best of the traditions they find. I think that is what is happening in England today. There is a continental feel about so many city centres; we enjoy drinking our cappuccinos *al fresco*; it seems that along with the packs of beer and cases of wine, we have imported other continental assets and to my way of thinking, that is all to the good. We will still refuse to talk to our neighbour on the tube home, but we are getting there.

One of the peculiarities about England as a whole is the wide range of weather systems in a relatively small country. This may explain why people here seem so obsessed with weather reports. TV channels usually offer a local regional weather report, followed almost immediately by a national forecast. It is fun to spot the differences between the two. I think the local weather channels are keen to extract the maximum out of every situation. So if it is going to rain, it is going to pour. If it is going to be sunny, it is going to be a scorcher. But it is not unusual for towns just a few miles apart to have quite distinct weather or even their own micro-climate.

While England is synonymous with rain, increasingly in the summer months, we are getting what passes for an English drought. The scale of this is nothing compared with Africa, but it means hosepipe bans in the garden, which makes headline news every year. The water companies are always portrayed as the culprits. They are accused of failing to repair leaks and failing to gather the water properly in the reservoirs. We are encouraged to cut down on baths and refrain from flushing lavatories too often. Invariably, these measures are introduced just as the heavens open and we get a wet spell, but I always like to look for the silver lining. The good news for England, as it basks in soaring continental temperatures, is that it means boom time, with tourists flocking here and increasingly people are taking extra holidays at home rather than flying off to the over-crowded beaches of Spain, where in all probability the temperatures are cooler! In just a few short weeks, the rain will always come again in England and the talk will be about floods.

For me, England still has the best climate in the world, even with all the solar or manmade disruptions. We seem to be having milder winters, longer springs and warmer summers—to my thinking, a perfect combination. I do not know whether the English are unique in their obsession with the weather, but I, for one, find it reflects the English character perfectly. It is a discreet *entrée* into a first meeting, non-threatening and non-invasive. The Japanese have a similar ritual with the exchange of business cards—much admiration of the card which, of course, is completely meaningless. Incidentally, I have found this is catching on with some European businessmen also. I was recently offered someone's card, held out in two hands like some religious offering. It will be some time, I suspect, before the English succumb to such vanities.

So in this topsy-turvy world, where England enjoys temperatures higher than the south of France and where the reduced rainfall is in danger of spoiling our traditional conversations, what are today's newcomers to England to make of it all and how should they steer a careful path through non-controversial discourse? There is no need to worry. The weather is always a safe bet when you first meet and now it has the added advantage of being a topic of conversation which has real meat if you choose to enter the global warming discussion. Everyone has an opinion—a bit like all the scientists who, of course, like nothing better than a debate.

Ultimately, of course, the weather will always be wrong for someone. Moaning about it is a national pastime—too hot, too cold, too wet, too dry—and one which will always remain. I am reminded once again about the eccentricities of the English. I believe the hotter it got, the late Enoch Powell, MP, would add another layer of clothing, which must have been something to behold as he invariably wore a three-piece suit. It seems he was insulating himself from the heat. I do not know what he did about umbrellas, but I like to think he had one which was tightly furled and never opened.

Never make the mistake of thinking the English do not care about serious topics, for they believe there is a time and place for everything. They do not like to discuss business at social gatherings—as opposed to the increasing number of so-called networking opportunities—but they do care deeply. Permit them a little moan about the weather because, beneath the façade of insouciance, lies a character of steel and determination of people who will back you to the hilt in times of trouble.

Good Old England—with its charming weather and changing attitudes!

16

Icons of England

To escape jury duty in England, wear a bowler hat and carry a copy of the Daily Telegraph.

John Mortimer

For nearly 60 years I have been impressed by how many iconic symbols of England and Englishness there are. When I first arrived in England, I was not aware that such icons existed, but after a short while I began to notice them. Now, I can see them everywhere. Of course, Her Majesty the Queen remains the most well-known and best recognised of all icons of England, but over the years I have been surprised by how many other iconic symbols there are. I believe there are more icons of England than there are of any other country—even my country of birth, India.

The first time I became aware of such iconic symbols was when I was working as an accountant at KPMG, the global accountancy and management consultancy firm. I would always take the trouble to look my best and dressed for work as a professional accountant would be expected to—suit and tie, polished shoes and a neatly folded handkerchief in my jacket pocket. It was the uniform of the professional, middle class, Englishman back in the 1960s and in one form or other, this suit and tie combination has remained the recognised standard dress for businessmen, much as a classic cut dress suit has been the standard attire for professional women in England.

However, I was struck by the way the partners at KPMG distinguished themselves from their staff through their dress code. Of course, the partners (at that time all the partners I had dealings with were men) wore their immaculately tailored, pin stripe Savile Row suits, but they were distinguished by the addition of two key elements which set them apart from the rest of us—a bowler hat and a tightly furled umbrella.

I had never seen a bowler hat earlier, so I had to learn quickly what it represented. It was, obviously, not a particularly practical piece of attire. I could not imagine that a bowler hat would offer much protection during inclement weather. I was also somewhat perplexed at the sight of a tightly furled umbrella, pressed under the partner's arm. It was obvious that the umbrella did not see much use and, what is more, the partners would carry their umbrellas even on the sunniest days when there was never a hint of rain in the weather forecast. So, what did all this mean?

I wanted answers and so I started to look around me and to use my powers of observation to make sense of it all. I am pleased to say that it did not take long for me to understand that the bowler and umbrella were symbols of authority, respectability, propriety and, above all, trustworthiness. My observations led me to appreciate that a suited, bowler-hatted gentleman represented all that was good and ethical about English society. Moreover, the bowler hat was the symbol of the City of London, the home of banking and insurance and, at the time I had arrived in England, the world leader in conducting ethical, honest and trustworthy business.

At this point, I have to say that this symbol has been rather tarnished in recent years, with various financial scandals and the global financial crisis of 2008, but the bowler hat and associated umbrella still stand out as internationally recognised symbols of England, even if fashion styles have changed so much that they are now rarely evident. However, you only need to view repeats of the 1960s television series *The Avengers*, which still enjoys international popularity, to realise how potent the symbols of the bowler and umbrella are—the lead character John Steed is rarely seen without them. In fact, in France, the title of the series was translated to *Chapeau melon et bottes de cuir* (*Bowler Hat and Leather Boots*) and in Germany the title was changed to *Mit Schirm, Charme und Melone* (*With Umbrella, Charm and a Bowler Hat*).

The iconic nature of the bowler hat got me thinking about the symbolism of other forms of headgear and how they reflected the class structures of England.

One of the most memorable television comedy sketches of recent years was the *Class Sketch*, performed in *The Frost Report* in 1966. This classic piece of satire featured John Cleese as an upper class businessman with a bowler hat and umbrella. Ronnie Barker played a middle class man in a Trilby hat, and Ronnie Corbett played a working class man wearing a flat cap. The very fact that no women appeared in the sketch was in itself a satirical statement on English society at the time, when men dominated all things social, cultural and economic.

As well as being a very funny sketch, it is most enlightening. The iconic nature of the hats symbolises the whole structure of English society at the time, in the simplest, yet most effective way. Once I understood this symbolism, I felt I was well on the way to understand more about my new homeland.

But, of course, I wanted to learn more and to discover whether there were any other icons which represented aspects of England and Englishness.

The English legal system is respected world-wide for its fair and balanced approach and for its wisdom in dispensing justice. The principles of English law go back to Magna Carta, which was drawn up in 1215. The assumptions of an individual's innocence until proven guilty and the right to be judged by a jury of one's peers are embodied in English law and have been adopted by countries throughout the world.

It did not take me long to find an iconic symbol which represented the English legal system—the statue of Lady Justice which sits on top of the Central Criminal Court (commonly known as the Old Bailey) in London. The key elements of the statue are that the lady depicted is blindfold and carries a set of scales in one hand and a sword in the other. This is, indeed, a powerful symbol, and although it is a classical image that is now seen in many countries, it is the one in London which makes the most lasting impression and which, to me, is the most iconic. Add to that image the iconic shape and styling of the English police officer's helmet and the wigs worn in court by judges and barristers, and I think you will agree with me that England's legal system is well served by iconic symbols.

Where else could I find iconic symbols of England? In this book, I mention the delight of having a glass of beer in an English country pub and, of course, the English country pub itself is as an iconic symbol of England. Where in the world, other than in England, would you find such simple, homely hospitality? Where else would you find the vast variety of images portrayed in English pub signs, many of which embody centuries of local and national history in their names and in the painted images they display?

My quest to uncover iconic symbols turned up many examples, ranging from sport (the weather vane of 'Old' Father Time at Lord's Cricket Ground in London; the Twin Towers of Wembley Stadium, now demolished, but ever present as an iconic symbol of the home of English football; strawberries and cream at Wimbledon) to transport (double decker buses; black taxi cabs; cars such as the Mini, Rolls Royce and the E-Type Jaguar; London's tube trains and the tube map and logo).

Everywhere, it seems, England has managed to brand itself successfully, so that any visitor or, as in my case, anyone settling in the country, immediately feels comforted in being surrounded by familiar images which have been projected around the world for many years.

That is not to say everything in England is as perfect as the iconic symbols may suggest. Far from it. I certainly do not recommend travelling on a London bus or the tube late on a Saturday night. All the positive promotion in the world will never disguise the fact that passengers who have over-indulged in alcohol and greasy take-away food can make you feel very uncomfortable if you happen to share a carriage or a bus seat with them.

Also, evidence of miscarriages of justice in the English legal system have rather tainted the notion of a faultless and fair legal system. Most recently there has been the controversy over the behaviour of the police in South Yorkshire in their handling of the disaster at Hillsborough stadium in 1989, when 96 football fans were crushed to death in tragic circumstances. But that has not affected my own belief in the broad values of the English way of life. If anything, it is most reassuring that a legal system can look in on itself and if it finds fault—even after 27 years—it is mature enough to admit there is something wrong and is prepared to take steps to put it right.

Of all the iconic symbols of England, and there are far too many to cover in just a single chapter of this book, perhaps the most elegant is the fine bone china tea cup and saucer. I have already mentioned elsewhere my love of the institution of taking afternoon tea in the luxurious surroundings of a top London hotel. I have also pointed out the great irony that tea itself originally came from India and China, only to become the national drink of England.

I suppose I should add to this the fact that the English establishment of tea plantations throughout the world represents a much more disturbing symbol of tea as a part of the English imperial history, rather than the elegant notion of it being the basis of genteel refreshment in the afternoon. But, despite the modern trend for re-writing history and rejecting old values, I have to reiterate that drinking tea is a pleasant, enjoyable and recuperative experience and, despite all the historical injustices which have been perpetrated in the name of trade and political expansion, it is an elegant and civilised activity.

As with so many icons, the tea cup and saucer are beginning to disappear from the scene, leaving just visual imagery in paintings, photographs and drawings, as a reminder of their iconic status. Few English people these days have time to relax over a cup of tea because, as we are told by the media, everyone leads a busy lifestyle.

In truth, few people now use actual china tea cups, favouring the more robust mugs and, when on the go, the horrendous styrofoam mugs. However, if you were to ask a visitor to England to list the top five iconic symbols that sum up England for them, you would be certain to find the tea cup and saucer still reigning supreme.

No relationship is ever perfect and that can certainly be said for my love affair with England. The symbolic icons of England present an ideal impression of what life is like, but beneath the surface, life is always different from its appearance. But like the Scales of Justice in the statue's hand, we have to look for a balance and in England life is just that, a balance between many opposing forces. In my 60 years in the country, I have been very fortunate to achieve a balance that has worked for me and for my family and I can only encourage other people to see England the way I do. It is not perfect, but it is a very charming and enjoyable place to live. It offers opportunities for anyone who is prepared to take advantage of them.

There is something special about a country that feels comfortable in being represented and recognised by a series of icons, even if some of them are well past their sell-by date. It is especially comforting to know that the country has a self-deprecating sense of humour and can certainly see the funny side when it makes its icons the objects of satire, as in the wonderful *Class Sketch* I mentioned earlier.

It is the fact that England does not take itself too seriously that makes me love the country and its people so much. I have a great deal to thank you for, England my love.

With Hon'ble Vice President of India

17

England My Love: Let Me Sum You Up!

England is never in a hurry because she is eternal.

Henryk Sienkiewicz

So how would you sum up life in England for a young person contemplating abandoning the land of their birth to live here for good? Once upon a time you would probably have said it tended to be a cold, wet country where the food was stodgy and bland, the people dressed badly and they were obsessed with football, darts and drinking flat beer. The Head of State was the Queen who had no power, did what one of two major parties in Parliament desired, but commanded huge respect. Not very appealing perhaps, but that was what I found it to be many years ago.

Today, much has changed and yet a lot has remained the same. It can be cold but the cold snaps seem to be shorter and the summers longer and hotter. The English are still sports mad but there is more on offer than just football. There are more varieties of beer, but foreigners would still consider them flat and the Queen, at the age of 90, God Bless Her, as the English would say, remains on her throne.

However, drag yourself away from the television and your computer games and you will find an extraordinarily diverse nation, changing radically from county to county despite all being wrapped up, so to speak, in a very small package—England.

Dialects are strikingly different across such a small country and when spoken in their broadest tongue, incomprehensible both to the foreigner and, in many cases, to the native English. There is music and theatre for every taste the length and breadth of the land, the food is as varied as the people and their characters and, yes, it has improved immeasurably.

The English still bristle at the very mention of Europe and, worse still, the European Union, although that may change now that the UK has voted to leave the EU. Yet the traffic between England and France is continuous, with influences being felt and enjoyed by both when it comes to wine, food and style. The bowler hat has all but disappeared and, at last, the English are taking some pride in their appearance, particularly among the young where even boys are becoming clothes conscious, rebelling against their parents' more casual dress sense.

London remains the throbbing heart of the country, although business is booming in the likes of Liverpool and Manchester. In part this is because of the high prices in London. England, and London in particular, is an expensive place to live. Still, I would say London is the most beautiful city in the world, with its wide open green spaces, ancient and modern architecture and diverse population.

England continues to punch above its weight; it refuses to give up its title as the financial centre of Europe, and it is, of course, a loud, some might say too loud, voice politically around the world.

What you may have read about the English landscape and countryside, with its quaint villages and country pubs, is still there, waiting to be discovered and, somehow, farmers still tend the fields and look after their flocks and herds to complete the picture postcard effect.

Like every society, there are great changes happening to all aspects of life in England, but there will probably always be that typical English stubbornness to resist too much change, too soon.

The greatest change to the country has been the influx of immigrants. The cheery, cheeky call from the workman hanging from the scaffolding is more likely to be in Polish these days than the Cockney I heard when I first arrived on these shores. What impact this will have on the true character and nature of the English, we will just have to wait and see. For years, though, the English have absorbed many influences and still somehow retained their true nature.

What is happening, though, is that large numbers of immigrants are not mixing with the indigenous community. Rather, they are sticking together, spending their working days and off-duty hours with their own, speaking their own language, eating their own food. Much of this is the result of economic migration, rather than the political migration that was so evident before the Second World War. Today, many immigrants come to England to work hard and earn good money, send some of it back to their families and then, after a few years, they choose to return to their homeland. London is the most international of all the cities, where some say more than 100 languages are spoken, but the capital is divided into sub-communities of Arabs, Jews, Chinese, Asians, Eastern Europeans and the rest.

Note the word 'divided'. All governments try to persuade us that we live in a mixed society, but there is little indication that the different communities do actually mix. It is like going into a sweet shop—there is every conceivable variety on sale, but you have to pick from different jars. I cannot help feeling that this is a mistake. In my view, not only should immigrants make an effort to escape these enclaves, but the English should try and drop their natural reserve and try socialising with their new guests, many who may soon be their fellow citizens.

We shall see how it unfolds. London claims to be a cosmopolitan city, but that suggests to me an integrated community and I do not think anyone would say that yet about it. In parts of

Leicester you could be in Mumbai, while a black, brown or Asian looking face would still cause a raised eyebrow or second glance in a country pub in, say, Sussex or Surrey.

I was given my break more than 50 years ago and seized my opportunity. Like Hollywood, England is a country where dreams can come true—just look at the ever growing number of millionaires in the Asian Rich list who have built major businesses in this country. But you have a choice when you arrive. You can keep your head down, stick with your own kind and build your own empire, or you can do all of that and get your head up and see what else this great nation has to offer. I chose the latter and actively went out to mix in the community, joined various clubs and organisations and, to all intents and purposes, chose to live like a true English citizen.

I firmly believe that that is the correct approach. It is also culturally more enriching. I went out of my way to find out more about this country, which has become my home and, in return, I was shown every possible courtesy and welcome. I decided long ago to cut the umbilical cord to India, not because I wanted to forget my own heritage but because I realised that if I wanted to make a new home for my family, not just an 'overseas office' from which I would one day return, I had to adopt and absorb my host country just as she was prepared to adopt and absorb me, without any reservation.

This is the real culture and character of the English. They are a tolerant, if slightly private, people, with a great and proud history and traditions going back centuries. Their heritage has grown and been enriched precisely because they were prepared to take in all peoples and their cultures. They have learned from these newcomers, adopted and adapted their strange foods, come to love their exotic musical instruments and, crucially, found room for them to settle.

In these few pages I have tried to paint a picture of a country which has its faults as well as its charms. It is a country which cannot be ignored. Shorn of its empire, it still manages to influence the world by influence and diplomacy. I read somewhere that the English had lost their empire but not their arrogance. By implication, England should not be throwing about its military weight in foreign lands. Maybe, maybe not, I am not passing judgement here, but the English do have courage, stoicism and their stubbornness. This bloody-mindedness has stood them in good stead for generations and many people in many countries have been grateful for that support.

Mistakes may have been made, even grave ones, down the years, but as someone once said, show me a person who has made no mistakes and I will show you a person who has never made anything.

I for one am proud to rejoice in England, warts and all. It is not a complicated place. By and large it applauds manners and courtesy, people still stand up and offer their places on the bus to others needier, they stand patiently in queues politely waiting their turn, they can be a little quiet and they still say 'please', 'thank you' and 'sorry' quite a lot.

However, we must be realistic and consider the challenges this great country faces. I do not mean international conflicts, but the pressures it must contend with internally. If immigrants follow my advice and throw themselves into all aspects of English life and truly integrate themselves with the indigenous community, then all will be well. But the trend does not seem to be going that way.

There is a certain pride—particularly it has to be said among the Indian community—in being self-sufficient. In one sense that is to be admired, but not if that same self-sufficiency is taken to an extreme, which it positively excludes or simply ignores the host nation. Quite apart from the fact that ultimately it will breed discontent, it makes no sense to ignore the beauty and riches of England. It is the equivalent of not talking to your neighbour—nothing can be gained from such discourtesy and everything can be gained by mutual cooperation and harmonious coexistence. The simple answer to most issues, big or small, is to talk and understand the other side's problems. Invariably the mountain does indeed turn out to be a molehill and, you never know, you might even enjoy each other's company.

This is the essential culture and nature of the English as I have found them through all my years here—a tough resilient lot, who seem to have a natural shyness and reserve instilled into them from birth but who, once you have pierced that protective shield, will be loyal and dependable friends.

When I first arrived here in the spring of 1959, I was unsure and apprehensive, like every newcomer to a foreign land must surely be. In those days there was an enormous amount of ignorance in some classes about what lay beyond the English Channel. Then, for a while, that ignorance turned to hostility, but by then I knew how England worked, I knew how to distinguish the racially motivated, ignorant minority from the educated, understanding majority and I knew that I was here to stay.

So should my advice to a potential immigrant be to come or to stay home?

I will have to be typically English and diplomatic about my answer and say that it must depend on the character of the individual. It is possible to get by as a scrounger, living off the generous welfare payments while they last, but this is a land where hard work is rewarded. When it comes to retirement, I can think of few more idyllic places to see out one's final years. If you are wise, you will endeavour to adopt the local ways without becoming a mimic—after all it was England and the English which attracted you in the first place. At least, do your hosts the courtesy of understanding and respecting their traditions and, in return, they will do you the courtesy of accepting, indeed welcoming, their new neighbour.

In time you too will be able to say, 'England—My Love!'

•••

That was the Journey...

- Falling in Love with England: Who Am I? 1
- The Legendary English Politeness 7
- Prejudice, the English Way 21
- The English Reserve 36
- The Meaning of English Family Life 42
- An Englishman's Home Is His Castle 51
- The Mysteries of the English Education System 65
- The English at Work 73
- The English Love of Sport 80
- The English Holiday Culture 87
- A New Era of English Eating and Drinking Habits 94
- The English National Health and Welfare 102
- England's Treasure: The Countryside 109
- The English Passion for Animals 115
- Where Would the English be without the Weather? 123
- Icons of England 130
- England My Love: Let Me Sum You Up! 137

GRATITUDE!

SK Ghai
Publisher

Paul Diner
Consulting Editor

Achal Paul
PR & Event Consultant

Jaya Lall
Secretarial & General Assistance

Simran Kaur
Secretarial & General Assistance

THE FAMILY